# digest
# of the
# Education Act
# 2005

John Fowler

Chris Waterman

Foreword by Helena Kennedy
Consultant editor, Alan Parker

Published in July 2005 by the
National Foundation for Educational Research
The Mere, Upton Park
Slough, Berkshire SL1 2DQ
www.nfer.ac.uk

Designed by Stuart Gordon
Layout by Helen Crawley

# Contents

# Quick guide to the Education Act 2005

# Foreword

A little over six months ago I was very pleased to write a foreword for the *Plain Guide to the Children Act 2004*. I am delighted that it became a best-seller, which demonstrates the value of a simple, but accurate, translation of a complex piece of legislation.

Less than six months later, in the 'wash-up' before the general election on 5 May, the Education Act 2005 received the royal assent. This is one of the longest Education Acts that has been introduced in recent years but within a matter of weeks we have a plain digest which distils the essential elements of the act and provides a valuable context for the rationale behind the legislation.

This digest, and the electronic guide to the act, will provide a plain English explanation of the act that is accessible to school governors, school staff and other professionals involved in the education service. It will also be of great value to undergraduate and post-graduate students of education - and also many solicitors and barristers who may find themselves involved in court work on the issues covered by the Act.

I am sure that this second commentary will be of enormous value and will join its predecessor on the best-seller list!

*Baroness Helena Kennedy, QC*

# About the authors

In a lifetime's commitment to improving the educational opportunities for all people, **John Fowler** has fulfilled a wide variety of roles including being a secondary school mathematics teacher, examinations manager, promoter of community education opportunities, parent, school, college and university governor, local authority officer, and local authority member. He currently undertakes management work in local government and writes on education policy and legislation. He was deputy head of education, culture and tourism and the Local Government Association from 1997 to 2002. John is a prolific writer. Recently his work has appeared in *Local Government Chronicle*, *Education Law Journal*, *NASG Governors' News* and the *Sunday Times*, to name just a few. Published books in the last three years in which John is either the author or a contributor include *Plain Guide to the Children Act 2004* (with C. Waterman), *School Improvement: making data work* (with S. Bird) and *What is the LEA for?* (ed. S. Whitbourn). John is also an Associate of The Education Network (TEN).

**Chris Waterman** worked as a primary teacher and taught basic skills in a further education college before spending eight years as an education officer in a London Borough. He has also worked for the Association of London Government, working on education, the arts and social services issues across the capital. He is currently Executive Director of ConfEd. Chris is Director of IRIS, the Institute for Research in Integrated Strategies, a new research institute and think tank. He is education advisor to Saving Faces: the Facial Surgery Research Foundation, director of e-strategix, a change management consultancy, and creative director of BWM-cabaret. A prolific writer and lecturer, Chris is Children's Services Editor of *Education Journal*. His recent publications include *Every School Matters*, *Plain Guide to the Children Act 2004* (with J. Fowler) and *Capital Idea*.

**Alan Parker** is a board member and Trustee of the NFER. He was also a contributor to *What is the LEA For?* (ed. S. Whitbourn). Alan took up the role of Schools Adjudicator on 1 March 2004. He was Director of Education in the London Borough of Ealing until July 2002 and since then has been working independently in the field of education policy and management. He has also worked within the education section of the Association of County Councils, as Principal Officer for Colleges in Surrey County Council, and was the Education Officer at the Association of Metropolitan Authorities from 1992 to 1997. He was an active member of the Association of Chief Education Officers and the Society of Education Officers, and was its President when it became ConfEd in 2002. He was also an advisor to the National Employers' Organisation for School Teachers and has served on a number of advisory and working groups on various aspects of education law and policy.

# Preface

The Education Act 2005 implements key aspects of the Government's New Relationship with Schools. This Digest provides an objective, section-by-section analysis of the Act in plain English, covering:

- what it says

- how it came about

- what happened in Parliament

- what is known about implementation in the context of the Government's developing education policies.

Information up to 20 June 2005 is included.

## Who should read this digest?

The Digest is aimed at:

- chief executives in local authorities

- directors of children's services

- lead councillors in local authorities

- senior education and children's services officers and advisors

- local authority legal teams

- schools forum members

- school leaders (headteachers, deputy and assistant headteachers)

- chairs of governing bodies and lead governors

- professional association representatives

- parent groups.

Further information on how the Act relates to the emerging children's services authorities (CSAs) can be found at the end of this introduction.

Although not a legal text, the Digest will be of interest to education lawyers. There is often a considerable wait before new education legislation appears in the standard education law texts. The Digest will provide background information to lawyers and alert them to the need to examine the primary legislation. Academics will find the Digest provides useful background information for policy research studies.

# Further reading: The Plain Guide to the Education Act 2005

The authors previously worked on the *Plain Guide to the Children Act 2004* (Waterman and Fowler, 2004), which provides easy access to the full text of the Act, with a 'plain' explanation placed alongside each section. The Education Act 2005 is nearly three times as long as the Children Act 2004, and the Digest describes the Act in a conveniently sized publication but without ready access to the text of the Act.

However, for those who want to read more and have access to the Act's text, an expanded version of the Digest is available as an online guide from the NFER (see www.nfer.ac.uk). Links are provided from the Act to the relevant section of the commentary and URLs are included where background information and references have been found from the internet.

# Wales

There remains a common basis to education law in England and Wales, but education policy and practice in the two countries has diverged since devolution in 1999. However, as the National Assembly for Wales does not have primary legislative powers, changes to legislation affecting Wales have to be made through Acts of the Westminster Parliament. About a third of the Act's sections deal specifically with Wales, and Wales-only provisions occur frequently in other sections.

An early decision was taken not to include the Wales legislation in this Digest. Inevitably, some comment on the Wales legislation does appear, frequently because existing legislation is amended to make it clear that it only applies to Wales. For example, the requirement to hold an annual parents' meeting is amended so that it only applies to Wales, with the effect that it no longer applies to England. The reader should be aware that the fact that this Digest states that the law has changed does not necessarily mean it has changed in Wales. It may mean that the law has changed in Wales but that the change does not have the same effect as in England.

# Nomenclature

Throughout the Digest, the following abbreviations are used for ease of reference:

s.      section

ss.     sections

para.   paragraph

Subsection, schedule and chapter are always written out in full. Note that s. 70(7) means subsection (7) of section 70.

# Feedback

The authors welcome feedback on the Digest. Queries are most welcome on the text. Comments about the usefulness of the text are also welcome as are suggestions about future publications on education legislation. Please email comments to John Fowler on john_fowler@btinternet.com.

# Thanks

Our first thanks go to you, the reader, for sustaining the tradition, established by local public service administrators, of seeking independent information on the law rather than simply relying on the interpretation provided by Ministers and civil servants.

We are grateful to the scrutiny work of Peers on the Bill during its passage through Parliament. Unfortunately, the truncated House of Commons Committee examination, caused by the declaration of the 5 May 2005 general election, did not give MPs the opportunity to conduct as rigorous an examination of the Bill as we would have liked. However, ministerial replies to questions have improved our understanding of the legislation and this is reflected in the text of this Digest.

The Digest relies heavily on the *Explanatory Notes to the Education Act 2005* (DfES, 2005b) (referred to as the *Explanatory Notes*) and the *Regulatory Impact Assessment* (RIA) published when the Bill was introduced into Parliament. We are indebted to the officials from the Department for Education and Skills (DfES) for their work in producing these documents and to the Bill team for clarifying, in discussion, a number of issues. We are also grateful to the House of Commons Library for the excellent *Research Paper 05/20* (GB.Parliament.HoC Library, 2005) on the Education Bill (9 March 2005).

We are indebted to the staff of NFER for their success in getting this book to market so soon after the Education Act 2005 received Royal Assent. In particular we wish to thank the Communications, Marketing and Information Services Department for their encouragement and perseverance. We particularly wish to thank our editorial consultant, Alan Parker.

Responsibility for the comments and judgements in this book remains with the authors. Although considerable experience of education legislation has been brought to bear on the Digest, the book does not purport to give definitive legal guidance or interpretation of the law – that is a matter for lawyers and the courts.

*John Fowler and Chris Waterman*

# Introduction

There has been a fashion for large Education Acts over the last 20 years and the 2005 Act is no exception. It is the fifth largest Education Act at 160 pages and of comparable size to the Learning and Skills Act 2000 (141 pages) and the Further and Higher Education Act 1992 (104 pages). However, the range of issues tackled is small with the majority of the legislation re-enacting earlier statutes with modifications.

## Passage through Parliament

The Act was introduced into the House of Lords on 30 November 2004 and received nine days of debate before reaching the House of Commons on 4 March 2005. The Bill received an unopposed second reading on 14 March, that is the Conservative and Liberal Democratic parties supported the principles behind the Bill without being committed to supporting all its provisions. The Bill spent only one day in Committee on 22 March, a remarkably short time for a lengthy piece of legislation. Following the declaration of the general election, all the remaining stages and Royal Assent took place on 7 April 2005.

## What's in the Act?

David Miliband MP, then Minister of State for School Standards at the DfES, wrote to local authorities when the Bill was published on 20 November 2004 under the curious heading '4th Session Education Bill', presumably to denote that it was a tidying-up piece of legislation at the end of a Parliament. The Minister described the Bill as:

> ... intended to simplify existing systems and reduce burdens by allowing schools in local authorities to focus on delivering high-quality education and care to communities.

Briefly, the Act seeks to:

- introduce a shorter, sharper school inspection system
- increase the number of competitions for new secondary schools
- extend the remit of the Teacher Training Agency to support the training and development of the whole school workforce

- introduce three-year budgeting for schools and channel all school expenditure through the DfES

- amend the law on school governance to 'remove duplication and clutter, free schools from unnecessary burdens and provide parents with better information to make informed choices about schools'.

## Raising standards: New Relationship with Schools and personalised learning

Frequently, the seeds of an education act are sown in the failures of previous acts. This is the case with the Education Act 2005. The momentum of school improvement having slackened by 2001, the Government sought and found a novel idea to breathe life into the task of raising standards, namely the promotion of 'innovation'. Although roundly lampooned by critics, this idea found its way onto the statute book in the Education Act 2002: an Innovation Unit was created at the DfES, and Ministers could disapply legislation to promote innovation in schools.

For a variety of reasons, including the appointment of a new Secretary of State (Charles Clarke) and Minister of State for School Standards (David Miliband), the Government's enthusiasm quickly waned. David Miliband did come back with other ideas to promote raising standards which have arguably been more successful. The first, 'personalised learning', was developed in 2003, although this did not require legislation. The second, the New Relationship with Schools, was launched at the North of England Conference in January 2004 and was followed in June 2004 by a more substantial paper *A New Relationship with Schools* (DfES and Ofsted, 2004a) building on the earlier Ofsted consultation paper *The future of inspection* (Ofsted, 2004). Further information on the new inspection arrangements can be found in the introduction to Part 1. The key elements of the New Relationship are described in the *Next Steps* document (DfES and Ofsted, 2005) are described below.

The New Relationship is much more than the new school inspection system. It is designed to build the capacity of schools to be effective learning institutions with rigorous self-evaluation, strong collaboration and effective planning for improvement. The 'Single Conversation' is central to the relationship, led by a 'School Improvement Partner' (SIP), where the school's self-evaluation is critical to the school's future development, which is periodically assessed through an Ofsted external inspection. The 'School Profile' is central to accountability to parents and the local community, and is based on data that is collected once electronically from schools and used many times. Communication between schools, local authorities and the DfES will be paperless, using all available electronic media.

## Five Year Strategy for Children and Learners

The package of reforms in *A New Relationship with Schools* was supplemented within a month by the DfES White Paper *Five Year Strategy for Children and Learners* (DfES, July 2004a) 'to sustain progress, with new and more radical reforms'. The White Paper attempted to integrate the separate DfES initiatives of children's services from the Children Act 2004, the New Relationship with Schools, and the development of skills in the older school and adult population. Specific initiatives were proposed, many of which did not require legislation to implement, for example, the commitment to establish 200 academies, giving every secondary school the opportunity to adopt a specialism and the expansion of popular schools. Specific new proposals that required legislation included three-year budgets for schools and mandatory competitions between potential promoters for new schools.

## A New Relationship with Schools: Next Steps

The DfES summarised progress on this broad agenda in *A New Relationship with Schools: Next Steps* (DfES and Ofsted, 2005), which brings together the relevant initiatives, although not those relating to school organisation and competitions for new secondary schools.

The *Next Steps'* vision for the new relationship is to:

- *build the capacity of schools to improve, with rigorous self-evaluation, stronger collaboration and effective planning for improvement*
- *enable talented school leaders to play a wider part in system-wide reform*
- *operate an intelligent accountability framework that is rigorous and has a lighter touch, giving schools, parents and pupils the information they need*
- *reduce unnecessary bureaucracy, making it easier for schools to engage the support they require without duplicative bidding, planning and reporting requirements*
- *improve data systems to put the most useful data on pupils' progress into the hands of schools and those who work with them*

- *secure better alignment between schools' priorities and the priorities of local and central government.*

*Our ultimate goal is to have a school system in which every child matters; in which attention is paid to their individual needs for education and well-being; and in which schools can develop the distinct ethos and approaches that maximise the potential of their pupils (page 4).*

The vision goes on to describe what the new relationship will do for parents, teachers, school governors, school leaders and local authorities.

The main changes are described in Table 1. The first three columns are taken from the *Next Steps* document, page 7. The last column gives the 2005 Act or other statutory reference.

**Table 1    Main changes made in the Education Act 2005**

| Key features | Old | New | 2005 Act |
|---|---|---|---|
| Inspection | 6–10 weeks' notice before an inspection | 2–5 days' notice | Section 5 and Ofsted's non-statutory *Framework for Inspecting Schools* (Ofsted, 2005a) |
| | Maximum 6-year interval between inspections | Maximum 3-year interval | |
| | Relatively large inspection teams visiting for a week | Small team visiting for no more than 2 days – around a quarter of current inspection weight | |
| Public accountability | Governors' annual report | *School Profile* | Section 103 and 104 |
| | Annual parents' meeting | | |
| School funding | 1-year funding aligned with financial year | 3-year funding aligned with academic years | Section 95 and Schedule 16 |
| | Over 20 separate grants | Fewer than 5 separate grants | Use existing powers in Section14, Education Act 2002 |

**Table 1    Continued**

| Key features | Old | New | 2005 Act |
|---|---|---|---|
| External support | Link advisors | Nationally accredited School Improvement Partners (SIP) working to local authorities | No specific statutory powers except through funding powers under Section 14, Education Act 2002. Amendment required to the Education (School Teacher Appraisal) (England) Regulations 2001 to allow SIP to appraise headteacher. |
| School self-evaluation and planning | Most schools undertake some form of evaluation, but not all, and not linked to planning and inspection | Self-evaluation as the starting point for inspection, planning, external relations | Ofsted's non-statutory *Framework for Inspecting Schools* (Ofsted, 2005a) |
| | Multiple accountabilities and support programmes | The 'single conversation' | No specific statutory powers except funding local authorities to provide SIPs under Section 14, Education Act 2002. |
| Data | Multiple surveys | School Census: data collected once, used many times data aligned | Existing data collection powers in 1996 and 2002 Education Act. |
| | Data on school performance not aligned across inspection, monitoring, planning | | Sections 113 and 114 enable electronic information on school workforce to be collected |
| Communications | Monthly batch of paper to all schools | Online ordering | DfES guidance including the Code of Practice on LEA School relationships (DfEE, 2001) |

# Implementing the Act

At the time of writing (June 2005) the DfES had not published a Commencement Order bringing into effect provisions of the Act. Some sections commence on enactment, although often it is a power to make regulations which comes into force immediately, and not the substantive provision. See commentary on s.125 (below) for further information.

## School workforce

The *Explanatory Notes* (DfES, 2005, para. 261) state that most of the provisions of part 3 on Training the School Workforce will come into effect on 1 September 2005.

## School inspection

The Ofsted website states that the new school inspection provisions in England (Part 1) will be introduced on 1 September 2005 (see, for example, Ofsted press release *Ofsted's new inspection arrangements*, 8 April 2005, www.ofsted.gov.uk/news/index.cfm?fuseaction =news.details&id=1685).

## School funding

DfES consultation on the new school funding arrangements (s. 101) to be introduced from April 2006, can be found at www.teachernet.gov.uk/management/schoolfunding/ consultation/.

## LEA targets in England

The DfES announced, through consultation on the guidance on the Children's and Young People's Plan, that the new plan will be supported by the statutory powers in s. 102 to require education targets to be set and agreed with the DfES. See paragraph 6, page 9 of DfES *Guidance on the Children and Young People's Plan* www.dfes.gov.uk/consultations/ downloadableDocs/Online%20Consultation%20Document.doc. New plans have to be in place by April 2006.

## School Profiles

DfES Consultation on *School Profiles* (s.104) states the intention of introducing them from September 2005. See www.dfes.gov.uk/consultations/conResults.cfm?consultationId=1241.

# Schools

The key tasks for schools are:

- preparing for the new inspection regime, particularly completing, and keeping up-to-date, the Self-Evaluation Form (part 1)

- considering the future of the school, if secondary, when the local authority brings forward school reorganisation proposals to meet falling rolls, and whether to stimulate interest in the school becoming an academy and/or a school with a religious character (part 2)

- noting the emphasis of the Training and Development Agency (TDA) on training the whole school workforce, and considering whether the school wishes to provide initial training for all members of the workforce in addition to teachers and higher level teaching assistants (part 3)

- managing the new three-year funding of budgets, including budgeting for the academic year, if confirmed following consultation (s. 101)

- noting that an annual parents' meeting no longer has to be held and considering how to improve relationships with parents, particularly in the light of the requirements of the new *School Profile* (ss. 103 and 104)

- considering whether the school wishes to put on courses of higher education (s.105)

- responding to the new admission arrangements for looked-after children: the statutory guidance on giving priority for school admission to children who are looked after by a local authority, as recommended in the Code of Practice on School Admissions, will become mandatory (s. 106)

- discussing with the LEA new arrangements for authorising free school lunches, etc. (ss. 110 to 112)

- preparing information about the school workforce for inclusion in the annual schools census (ss. 114 to 115)

- making use of the power to require excluded pupils to attend alternative provision (ss. 115 and 116).

## Local authorities/children's services authorities – general

The Act gives local authorities major opportunities to demonstrate local leadership over a range of school-based issues. Local authority advisory and support staff will need to work with the local authority appointed School Improvement Partners to help schools develop their competence in self-assessment in preparation for the new inspection regime (part 1, particularly s. 5). The halving of the inspection cycle from six years to three will mean that in any given period, the local authority will be in receipt of twice the number of inspection reports. Local authorities will have much more up-to-date information about the quality of education in their maintained schools. Ofsted states that the schools in the trials of the new inspection system managed the self-evaluation process well and that there was no increase in the proportion of schools found to be causing concern. Local authorities will wish to monitor how many of their schools are found to be causing concern under the new inspection arrangements, especially the application of the new 'requires significant improvement' category.

The challenge of secondary school reorganisation in a period of falling rolls, at the same time as managing a substantial capital injection into the building stock, will be made harder by the competition requirements in part 2 of the Act. Local authorities will have to plan for an additional lead-in time before reorganisation can be brought about. The uncertainty that already exists for parents, pupils and staff in schools subject to reorganisation will be increased by a public debate not only about the future structure of schooling but also about the ownership and mission of successor schools. All those involved will have to engage with the competing possibilities of remaining a local authority community school, going independent in the form of an academy, or adopting a religious character, which staff members and parents of existing pupils may find incompatible with their own beliefs.

Local authorities will wish to welcome the new role for the TDA and work with schools to provide training for all members of the school workforce, including the initial training of new members of the workforce (part 3).

Perhaps the biggest challenge for local authorities in the Act is the new school funding arrangements and the consequential effect on other local authority services when approximately half of the current local government funding is transferred to the new Dedicated Schools Grant (DSG). It is very unlikely that the new funding arrangements will exactly replicate the current distribution of non-school expenditure and some local authorities will find themselves significant losers. Coinciding, as this will, with turbulence arising from council tax revaluation, there will need to be difficult decisions taken over cuts in services or the raising of local taxes. Local authorities will retain responsibility for distributing the DSG to schools, which may present additional challenges reconciling new regulations, including the minimum funding guarantee, with former local formulae and future needs (s. 101)

Local authorities will need to develop targets for the Children and Young People's Plan to meet the requirements of s. 102.

Local authorities will have an important task in developing the competence of school governing bodies on the information required for the new *School Profile*. They will also have a role in enhancing accountability to parents by ensuring *School Profile* information is readily available via local internet access and printed publications (ss. 103 and 104).

Achieving a fair balance between the needs of children in local authority care to have the best education and the concerns of schools has been a challenge to many local authorities. Section 106 provides an opportunity for local authorities once and for all to get the admission arrangements for these children right.

The new arrangements to confirm the eligibility for free school meals (FSM) found in ss. 110 to 112 will be welcomed by local authorities.

Likewise, the streamlined and automated data collection arrangements for the school workforce, and the abolition of Form 618g, should be beneficial to staff, provided appropriate arrangements for data security are put in place (ss. 113 to 114).

The new provisions enabling, and in effect requiring, school governing bodies to require excluded pupils to attend educational provision will be appreciated by local authorities who, no doubt, will wish to offer schools appropriate assistance. The sanctions that local authorities can use against parents who fail to ensure that their children attend such provision should prove useful (ss.115 and 116).

## Local authorities/children's services authorities – Every Child Matters

Many colleagues have expressed surprise to the authors that the term 'local education authority' (LEA) is used throughout the Act. The Act has 174 occurrences of the term 'local education authority', or its variants: 'LEA' and 'local education authorities'. This compares to five occurrences of the term 'children's services authority', all in ss.113 and 114.

There is a perception that the Children Act 2004 abolished the LEA and replaced it with the children's services authority. In statutory terms, the Children Act 2004 did no such thing. The CSA sits above the LEA as a convenient statutory vehicle to describe those local authorities that have education and children's social services functions. In addition, the CSA is given separate functions by the Children Act 2004, for example the duty to promote cooperation (s. 10), the duty to have a Children and Young People's Plan (s. 17), and the duty to appoint a Director of Children's Services (s. 18) and a Lead Member (s.19).

Part of the confusion lies in the different uses of the term 'local education authority' and its variants. The use in legislation has to be distinguished from its use in everyday parlance.

Legislation uses the term LEA as a way of describing a local authority's education functions or 'a principal local authority exercising its functions under the Education Acts and other relevant legislation" (Whitbourn *et al.*, 2004, p.1). The electronic version of the standard text on education law, *Butterworth's Law of Education*, records (in mid-June 2005) 3285 occurrences of the term 'local education authority', or its variants, in primary legislation and the commentary on the legislation. It is quite possible that for nearly all of these occurrences the term 'children's services authority' could be substituted for 'local education authority'. Making such changes to legislation would clearly be a massive undertaking, as each case would have to be separately examined. This is not the case for children's social services where the local authority functions are listed as a schedule to the Local Authority Social Services Act 1970, where the complete list of functions is recorded on a few sides of A4.

The term 'local education authority' is still a working term used in local government to describe what local government does for education and was, and remains, widely used to denote the former 'education department' as the administrative arm of the local authority responsible for education. (Legislation is itself not entirely exempt from this confusion - see Whitbourn *et al.*, 2004, pp.18, 19.) It is still clearly a term fixed in the minds of teachers, parents and anyone else dealing with publicly funded education.

An example of the confusion between the two usages of the term can be shown in a speech by the then Chairman of the House of Commons Education and Skills Select Committee (Barry Sheerman MP) who, at the second reading of the Education Bill that became the 2005 Act, pronounced that 'local education authorities no longer exist' and then went on to ask why the Bill contained so many references to the term 'local education authority'. (Commons Hansard, 14 Mar 2005, column 54). In statutory terms he was wrong, but in every day local government and education parlance, he had a point.

The Act is also charged frequently with undermining the Every Child Matters agenda because of the Government's drive to boost the autonomy of schools. However, the authors contend that this view is derived from a mistaken understanding of the Act. The major innovation in the legislation, as far as school practice is concerned, is the new school inspection system, and the Act deliberately forces schools to address the Every Child Matters agenda through the inspection arrangements (s. 5). Schools will be assessed externally by Ofsted every three years on their contribution to the well-being of pupils. The language of Her Majesty's Chief Inspector's (HMCI) reporting duty and the focus of school inspection links directly into the task of children's services authorities to improve the well-being of all children. If it is found that the 'five outcomes' are not being achieved because the school is failing to cooperate with the wider provision of children's services, then the school may be found to be 'causing concern'. If it is true that there is a modern English education tradition of only valuing what is assessed, this Act represents a brave attempt to secure the measurement of important, but previously unrecognised, aspects of the service.

The Act also recognises that the whole school workforce has a contribution to the education, development and well-being of children. The TDA is charged in its funding, curricula and standards work to ensure that the school workforce contributes to the well-being of children (s. 75) and data will be collected on the contribution of the whole school workforce, be they educators or carers, to the work of schools (ss. 113 and 114).

The one charge against the Act which we believe can be substantiated is that it still leaves major areas of legislation, and the resultant practice, untouched by the Every Child Matters agenda. One area where the Government has announced progress, through the curious device of the Chancellor's Budget speech on 15 March 2005, is in the integration of inspection services and the transfer of the inspection of children's services from the Commission for Social Care Inspection (CSCI) to Ofsted. Bringing the CSCI's expertise to bear directly on the new school inspection arrangements could prove to be enormously beneficial to children.

No announcements have, however, been made on other areas of local government and education practice. For example, the large number of statutory orders that local authorities can either make, or apply to the courts to make, about children, their education and care, and their families remain untouched. Another important area is how local authorities budget for, and record, expenditure on children. If local authorities are going to provide integrated services then the Government must amend the legislative constraints on, for example, the s. 52 statement of the School Standards and Framework Act (SSFA) 1998, which requires local authorities to record expenditure made only under LEA functions. A developed s. 52 statement is needed, which covers children's social services and other valuable services for children and young people such as play, leisure, libraries, culture, music, road safety, sports and youth democracy. The mistake of the Children Act

2004 was to presume that integrated services can be achieved by the production of a plan, requiring a single point of political and managerial accountability through the appointment of a 'lead member' and a director of children's services. It is very difficult to integrate services unless the expenditure streams, and their reporting arrangements, are also integrated. Otherwise the bureaucracy becomes excessive and frontline workers do not see the benefits of changing practice; and may even suffer perverse incentives to avoid providing better integrated services to improve the well-being of all children.

## The future

The relentless pace of legislative change has not slackened, and will not do so, as judged by the Queen's Speech given on 17 May 2005. There will be four Bills in which the DfES has a hand, including another major education bill. NFER and the authors look forward again to another opportunity to record in plain language the legislative changes affecting the care and education of children and young people.

# Part 1 School inspections and other inspections by school inspectors

## New school inspection system – overview

Brief details of the new school inspection system have already been given in the Introduction. The Ofsted consultation document *The Future of Inspection* (Ofsted 2004, para. 32) stated that:

> *Ofsted's priorities are to ensure that inspection delivers the things that parents, schools, government and other stakeholders expect: higher standards, continual improvement, and greater opportunities for all children. With these priorities in mind, the key objectives of a new approach would be to:*
>
> - *introduce shorter, less onerous, more frequent inspections*
>
> - *reduce significantly the notice of inspection given to providers*
>
> - *ensure closer contact between HMI and independent inspectors*
>
> - *incorporate all aspects of children's services provided by the school.*

These priorities have now been translated into legislation through the Education Act 2005.

## Key features of the new inspection system

Table 2, taken from *A New Relationship with Schools* (DfES and Ofsted, 2004a), shows the principal changes to the school inspection system. The final column shows the changes following the Education Act 2005. The Draft Non-statutory *Framework for Inspecting Schools* is found at www.ofsted.gov.uk/publications/index.cfm?fuseaction =pubs.displayfile&id=3861&type=pdf, dated 9 March 2005.

**Table 2     Principal changes made to the school inspection system**

| Current system – School Inspection Act 1996 | New system in DfES/OfSTED document *A New Relationship with Schools* (June 2004) | New system following the Education Act 2005 |
| --- | --- | --- |
| 6–10 weeks' notice before an inspection | 2–5 days' notice | Draft non-statutory *Framework for Inspecting Schools* (Ofsted, 2005a, paras 19 and 23). Most schools will receive 2 days' notification |
| Relatively large inspection teams visiting for around a week | Small teams visiting for no more than 2 days – around a quarter of the current inspection weight | Draft non-statutory *Framework for Inspecting Schools* (Ofsted, 2005a, para.10) |
| A maximum 6-year interval between inspections | A maximum 3-year interval | School Inspection Regulations under s. 5(1)(a). All schools to receive first inspection under new arrangements by 1 August 2009, and thereafter within three years after the end of the last school year in which inspected, that is the interval could be nearly 4 years in practice. |
| Inspections cover:<br>– standards and quality of education<br>– leadership/management<br>– spiritual, moral, social and cultural development | Inspection reports will, as now, cover:<br>– standards and quality of education<br>– leadership/management<br>– spiritual, moral, social and cultural development within the context of the 5 outcomes set out in Every Child Matters | Section 5(2) |
| Most schools undertake some form of evaluation, but it is not structured across all schools nor part of the inspection process | Inspection evidence will start from a school's self-evaluation | Draft non-statutory *Framework for Inspecting Schools* (paras 12 and 13) and Ofsted publication *A new Relationship with Schools: Improving Performance through School Self-Evaluation* (DfES and Ofsted, 2004b). HMCI will have to keep the Secretary of State informed as to the extent to which schools are developing rigorous internal procedures of self-evaluation under s. 2(1)(g). |
| Collection of a wealth of information – extensive use of lesson observation | Focus on core systems and key outcomes, informed by lesson observation and other indicators of pupils' progress – self-evaluation evidence at the heart of the inspection system | Draft non-statutory *Framework for Inspecting Schools* (Ofsted, 2005a, paras 20 to 22) |

**Table 2 Continued**

| Current system – School Inspection Act 1996 | New system in DfES/OfSTED document A New Relationship with Schools (June 2004) | New system following the Education Act 2005 |
|---|---|---|
| Inspections usually conducted by registered inspectors | HMI leading many inspections and involved in all inspections | All inspections conducted by HMCI under s. 5(1). Draft non-statutory *Framework for Inspecting Schools* (Ofsted, 2005a, para. 16) indicates that inspection providers (private companies supplying additional inspectors) will assemble teams. New rules on qualifications of Ofsted additional inspectors found in Schedule 1 |
| Registered inspectors responsible for some inspection reports, HMI for others | HMCI accountable for all inspection reports | HMCI responsible for all inspections under s. 5(1). |
| Detailed and relatively lengthy (30+ pages) inspection reports produced | Short, sharp reports (around 6–12 pages) focused on key outcomes with clearer recommendations for improvement | Draft non-statutory *Framework for Inspecting Schools*, (Ofsted, 2005a, paras 44 and 45) |
| Reports produced within 40 days of the inspection event | Most reports will be with the governing body, at least in draft, by the end of the week of the inspection | Draft non-statutory *Framework for Inspecting Schools*, (Ofsted, 2005a, para. 46). If the school is a cause for concern, schools will be sent a draft report under s.13, and the draft School Inspection Regulations gives the governing body five working days to review the report. HMCI must consider any comments they make. |
| Schools required to prepare a separate post-inspection action plan | Schools feed their intended actions into the school development plan | Draft non-statutory *Framework for Inspecting Schools* (Ofsted, 2005a, para. 52) |
| Various categories of schools causing concern – special measures, serious weaknesses, underachieving and inadequate sixth forms | Rationalised system with two categories – special measures and improvement notice | Section 44 prescribes two categories of schools causing concern: requiring special measures and requiring significant improvement. |

There are two key features of the new system that are not related to the process issues of timing, number of inspectors, length of report, etc. These are the self-evaluation and who does the inspecting.

# Self-evaluation and the self-evaluation form

Basing school inspection on self-evaluation and in particular the need for schools to write and keep up to date the self-evaluation form (SEF) is a major change. The SEF does ask challenging questions of schools. The draft secondary school form, found at www.ofsted.gov.uk/schools/sef.cfm, is 37 pages long. Although much of the information is factual and can be completed electronically, schools still have to answer questions such as 'How good is the quality of teaching and learning?' and 'What is the overall effectiveness and efficiency of leadership and management?' The answers have to be based on evidence that can be inspected. The SEF takes into account the requirements of Every Child Matters and the five outcomes within it. (See s. 2, page 11 for the 'five outcomes'.

Ofsted sums up the move to self-evaluation in the following terms (taken from www.ofsted.gov.uk/ofsteddirect/index.cfm?fuseaction=displayarticle&articleid =28&issueno=2):

*Ofsted believes that schools are best placed to recognise their own strengths and weaknesses. This is why we are introducing a new inspection system which puts more onus on a school to be proactive and demonstrate to inspectors that it can not only diagnose where its strengths and weaknesses are, but more crucially, do something about improving and developing them. Ofsted can then focus its inspections on the school's evaluation of itself and therefore make inspection sharper and more helpful. At the same time, we can lighten the burden of inspection on schools.*

*The self evaluation form (SEF) is at the heart of the new inspection arrangements – it serves as the main document when planning the inspection with the school, and is crucial in evaluating the quality of leadership and management and the school's capacity to improve.*

*The SEF asks schools*

- *to evaluate their progress against an inspection schedule*

- *to set out the main evidence on which this evaluation is based*

- *to identify strengths and weaknesses*

- *to explain the action the school is taking to remedy the  weaknesses and develop the strengths.*

Ofsted have also published a full description of how self-evaluation works with model answers. *A New Relationship with Schools: Improving Performance through School Self-Evaluation* (DfES and Ofsted, 2004b) can be found at www.ofsted.gov.uk/publications/index.cfm?fuseaction=pubs.displayfile&id=3862&type=pdf.

## Who will do the inspecting?

The other major change in the new arrangements is abolition of the Registered Inspector, a person who led school inspections, with assistant inspectors, under contract to Ofsted. In future, inspections will be led by HMI or 'additional inspectors' (see commentary on Schedule 1 below for more information on additional inspectors). The arrangements as announced by Ofsted press release *Ofsted's new inspection arrangements* (Ofsted, 2005b), may be found at: www.ofsted.gov.uk/news/index.cfm?fuseaction=news.details&id=1685, and are as follows.

> *The Education Act 2005 provides that HMCI is responsible for the inspection and the report, and this responsibility will be delivered by the involvement of HMI in all inspections, working in a regional structure. The majority of secondary school inspections, and a proportion of primary and special school inspections will be led by HMI. The regional structure is now in place, based on three regions – North, Midlands and South – with offices in Manchester, Nottingham and Bristol respectively. Policy will be managed from Ofsted's London headquarters in Alexandra House. […]*

> *In order to deliver inspections regionally, we have decided that we will work with private sector inspection providers on a regional basis. The decision to work with the market and their inspectors is a deliberate choice; other options available could have been to carry out all inspections using HMI and directly employed additional inspectors as we currently do in school improvement work. Ofsted felt very strongly that partnership with the private sector will help to deliver more effectively and at better value for money. We are able to say that the competitive tender process has allowed us to secure service for the next four years from five companies arranged across the regions and at savings of about £15m each year.*

> *The five companies are as follows: in the North, Nord Anglia Education plc (www.nasis.co.uk) and CfBT (www.cfbt.com); in the Midlands, Cambridge Education Ltd (www.camb-ed.com) and Tribal Education Ltd (www.tribaleducation.co.uk); and in the South, Prospects Learning Services Ltd (www.prospects.co.uk) and Tribal Education Ltd (www.tribaleducation.co.uk).*

*We expect these inspection providers to begin recruitment and training for the inspectors who will undertake the inspections alongside HMI; each inspector will be supported by HMI on their first inspection and all the inspections will be quality assured.*

The role of the Registered Inspector and the need to change the arrangements was much debated by the House of Lords. The Government was forced to agree significant changes to the role of additional inspectors. See the commentary on schedule 1 on page 9.

Baroness Andrews, on behalf of the Government, explained (Lords Hansard, 11 January 2005, col 153 to 155) the need for change.

*The* [registered and assistant] *inspectors have been recruited from many different backgrounds over the years. [...] But regardless of where they come from, the inspectors have in common an ability to produce the standards necessary to lead and manage a school inspection. [...] They must be able to demonstrate the experience and skills for the phase of education they intend to inspect. [...] Being on the register has simply provided a status that means that the individual can be trusted to undertake a school inspection. [...] To get on to the register an individual must initially demonstrate fitness to practise. However, the register has not been an indicator of how good an inspector is at delivering inspections to the required standard. That is reflected in the fact that being on the register is, paradoxically, no guarantee of employment or regular participation. It is possible to be on the register without intending to inspect regularly, and some inspectors may make only three or four inspections a year. For some, inspector status has been a passport to other forms of employment.*

*Moreover, registered inspectors are not a part of Ofsted; they are employed by a range of contractors who are themselves independent of Ofsted. Many of them operate on self-employed terms as autonomous units. The chief inspector has little or no say on which individuals are used to conduct which inspections; he can only require that they meet the specification for a tender exercise. [...] So in making the decision to replace the system of a register of inspectors with a greater role for HMIs in the inspection and reporting process, we have been motivated by the intention to enhance the inspectorate system and to enrich the professional development opportunities and systems that will ensure that quality, performance and accountability are improved. [...] [The] new system creates a new relationship between Ofsted and the providers which is based on collaboration and teamwork rather than regulation. [...]*

*Every additional inspector, HMI or not, and regardless of skill, competence or experience, will have to undergo the same training to implement the new system as HMIs.*

*They will be trained together to deliver the new framework. […] There will be a scheme of continuous performance assessment that will apply to all inspectors and inspections and set out the principles for quality in terms of new inspections and the principles for performance management. […] Performance management will be undertaken on a team basis. Ofsted and RISPs [Regional Inspection Service Providers] will share responsibility for HMIs and contracted inspectors. They will work to key performance targets. There will be a continuous process that feeds individual professional improvement and development. There will be no new entry test for additional inspectors but there will be a clearer, tighter framework for continuous professional monitoring and improvement. […] [There will be] clearer accountability and a greater role for HMIs. The independence of the registered inspectors left him or her entirely accountable for the system and, sometimes, as we all know, at war with the HMI who was powerless to intervene to change things. That will be replaced by the chief inspector who will authorise inspectors who are fit to practise and remove that right if necessary. […]*

*[In future, additional inspectors] will all have to meet the criteria that HMIs set out and on which we have been working. The criteria will be much nearer to those that we would expect for HMIs themselves. Inspectors will have to demonstrate the ability to meet those criteria in the inspection process, the evaluation of evidence, the choice of evidence and the quality of judgments. HMCI will be directly responsible for ensuring that they are all up to the job.*

*[…] At the moment a registered inspector, independent of Ofsted, can publish a report without the approval of the chief inspector. Even in the most serious cases, where he feels that special measures are warranted, an inspector could in theory publish a report although the chief inspector disagreed with the judgment. That means that at present Ofsted can make changes to inspection reports only with the agreement of the registered inspector. As a result, schools have in some cases been left frustrated, dissatisfied with the judgment and unable to have their concerns addressed swiftly and helpfully. […]*

*Under these new arrangements, inspectors will not have free-standing powers to issue reports as all reports will be issued by the chief inspector. Since a key purpose of the register of inspectors is to confer the right on those inspectors to issue reports in their own right, the requirement for a register becomes redundant. However, there is another element. A simple fitness to practise register will not be sufficient to meet the new demands which we are building into the system – a more comprehensive system with*

*performance management, a quality assurance system and a process which is being*
*tested successfully in the pilot schemes at present. […] Removing the register does not*
*remove the independence which is reflected in the market operation of the provider*
*system. The experience of contractors – who will be fewer but not less competitive –*
*will be used to best effect working in partnership with Ofsted. Contractors will have a*
*vital part to play. They will have to recruit inspectors and demonstrate that those*
*recruits meet the criteria defined by Ofsted, matching the competencies expected of*
*HMI. HMI will monitor the process and ensure that they are of consistently high qual-*
*ity. […] Under the new system, given the likelihood of far fewer inspectors, many*
*individuals are likely to become employed by these contractors with the employment*
*protection that that brings. Individuals who feel aggrieved will be able to call upon the*
*full range of employment protection laws and other services. […] If contractors have,*
*or HMCI has, doubts in future about an inspector's competence they will simply be*
*able to cease to use that inspector, without a time-consuming deregistration process.*
*They are not able to act arbitrarily. There will be arrangements to follow up com-*
*plaints from inspectors. But the system will be much more responsive to evidence of*
*quality.*

# Summary of part 1

In part 1 of the Education Act 2005 the legislative basis of school inspection is detailed, and the School Inspections Act 1996 is repealed and replaced by 63 sections and nine schedules of the Education Act 2005.

Chapter 1 establishes Her Majesty's Inspectorate (HMI) of Schools in England, and the duty to inspect schools, chapter 2 describes what happens to inspection reports and the procedure when a school is found to be a cause of concern, chapters 3 and 4 apply to Wales, chapter 5 contains the new definition of a school causing concern, chapter 6 deals with religious education inspections, LEA inspection powers and amendments to the inspection arrangements for child minding, day care and nursery education and inde-pendent schools, and chapter 7 contains miscellaneous provisions.

## A note on the position in Wales

This part represents almost half the 2005 Act's 128 sections. However, 31 sections and four schedules apply only to Wales. There are only 20 sections and one schedule that apply only to England. The main common provisions relating both to England and

Wales are the definitions of schools causing concern (s. 44) and the LEA power to inspect maintained schools for a specific purpose (s. 51). After a long period of consultation, Estyn, the office of Her Majesty's Inspectorate for Education and Training in Wales, introduced in September 2004 a new inspection system based on a Common Inspection Framework covering schools, further education colleges, LEAs and nursery education. The new system was based on the School Inspections Act 1996. In view of its recent introduction, the Education Act 2005 re-enacts relevant parts of the School Inspections Act as Wales-only provisions. There are some new Wales-only provisions mainly relating to new powers for the National Assembly of Wales, including the establishment of an Advisory Committee (s. 22), a role in the appointment of the Chief Inspector (s. 23) and a power to apply the England-only legislation to Wales without recourse to the Westminster Parliament (s. 62).

# Chapter 1: school inspectors and school inspections: England

Chapter 1 established Her Majesty's Inspectorate of Schools in England, and the duty to inspect schools. Section 1 and schedule 1 establish Her Majesty's Inspectorate of Schools in England; section 2 describes the functions of HMCI; section 3 contains reporting requirements and section 4 re-enacts the powers of entry to carry out inspections.

## Section 1: Her Majesty's Inspectorate of Schools in England

The offices of Her Majesty's Chief Inspector of Schools (HMCI) and Her Majesty's Inspector of Schools (HMI) are established as Crown appointments. HMI are members of HMCI's staff. HMCI is appointed for a term of up to five years but may be removed from office on grounds of incapacity or misconduct. Previous post-holders are not barred from reappointment. The position remains the same as that created by section 1 of the School Inspections Act 1996 (SIA, 1996).

## Schedule 1: Her Majesty's Chief Inspector of Schools in England

There are substantial changes in schedule 1 compared with the equivalent provision (also schedule 1) of the SIA 1996 on the role and function of 'additional inspectors'. HMCI has long had a power to appoint 'additional inspectors' to undertake inspection work, for example when specific skills or knowledge are required for an inspection. Under the new school inspection system, HMCI does not have to maintain a list of registered inspectors (see section 2 below) and the majority of inspection personnel will be 'additional inspectors' (AIs) provided by private sector companies, referred to as 'inspection service providers' in schedule 1(2)(6).

Schedule 1(1) enables HMCI to appoint staff other than HMI. This will include administrative staff as well as directly employed AIs. Schedule 1(2) enables HMCI to arrange for AIs to assist in inspection work. They do not have to be employed by HMCI.

Several Government-led changes to this schedule were made in response to pressure from opposition Peers in the House of Lords, who were seeking greater accountability of AIs in the new inspection system.

HMCI must ensure that AIs 'have the necessary qualifications, experience and skills' and HMCI must publish a statement of what this means for AIs who are not on his/her staff. The statement must contain the standards that AIs are required to meet and the skills that they are required to demonstrate (schedule 1(2)(4)). HMCI must require any 'inspection service provider' to comply with a similar set of qualifications and experience standards (schedule 1(2)(5)). When using an inspection service provider, HMCI must publish a list of names given to him/her by the inspection service provider of persons who may be used as additional inspectors (schedule 1(2)(6)). Additional inspectors acting within the authority conferred by HMCI have the powers of an HMI (schedule 1(2)(7)), but HMCI cannot authorise an AI to conduct a school inspection under s. 5 (see page 14) unless the inspection is supervised by an HMI or the AI has previously conducted an inspection to the satisfaction of an HMI (schedule 1(2)(8)). Presumably, an AI can become qualified to lead inspections through 'on the job training' by HMI.

Schedule 1(5) enlarges HMCI's power to delegate functions to HMI, other members of HMCI's staff and any additional inspector. This is subject to the limitations on the responsibilities of AIs (see note on schedule 1(2)(8) in the previous paragraph) and schedule 1(5)(3), which requires that an inspection report finding that special measures are required must be personally authorised by HMCI or an HMI specifically authorised to do so.

## Section 2: functions of Her Majesty's Chief Inspector of Schools in England

The functions of HMCI found in section 2 are broadly similar to those in the equivalent section (also s. 2) of the SIA 1996. The main exception is that HMCI does not have to establish and maintain a register of inspectors eligible to conduct school inspections under s.10 of the SIA 1996 Act. The other SIA provisions on registered inspectors will be repealed, as far as

England is concerned, by s. 60 of the 2005 Act (see below). See schedule 1 (above) for the role of additional inspectors (AIs) who will conduct inspections with HMI.

HMCI's general duty to keep the Secretary of State informed is enlarged. Four requirements that appeared in the SIA 1996 are re-enacted unchanged. These are that HMCI must keep the Secretary of State informed about:

- the quality of the education provided by schools in England

- the educational standards achieved in those schools

- the quality of the leadership in and management of those schools, including whether the financial resources made available to those schools are managed efficiently

- the spiritual, moral, social and cultural development of pupils at those schools.

To these the Government added:

- the extent to which the education provided by schools in England meets the needs of the range of pupils

- the contribution made by schools in England to the well-being of their pupils.

Although not explicitly stated in parliamentary debate or elsewhere, the first of these is probably intended to ensure that HMCI advises the Secretary of State on the education of all identifiable groups being educated in schools, particularly vulnerable children. The second requirement relates to the Every Child Matters agenda and has to be read in conjunction with the definition of 'well-being' found in section 12 (interpretation) of the 2005 Act, which refers back to section10(2) of the Children Act 2004. In other words, HMCI has to advise the Secretary of State about the contribution schools make to the 'five outcomes' for improving the well-being of children, namely:

a) physical and mental health and emotional well-being

b) protection from harm and neglect

c) education, training and recreation

d) the contribution made by them to society

e) social and economic well-being.

Following Government defeats in the House of Lords two more requirements were added:

- the extent to which schools in England are developing rigorous internal procedures of self-evaluation

- the behaviour and attendance of pupils at schools in England.

The first was added because of concerns about how schools will manage the self-evaluation procedures that will be at the heart of the new school inspection system, and the second because of general concerns about the behaviour of pupils in schools, especially in the pre-general election period.

Section 2(2) requires HMCI, when asked by the Secretary of State, to give advice on educational matters, and to inspect and report on any school, or class of schools. The reason for the Secretary of State's power to ask for a named school to be inspected is obvious, but the reference to 'class of schools' is mainly to enable the Secretary of State to ask for thematic inspections, for example of information technology in secondary schools.

HMCI must keep under review the extent to which LEAs and school governing bodies comply with the inspection regime. It can be inferred from this provision that HMCI has a duty to ensure that the inspection regime is not burdensome. HMCI can advise the Secretary of State on any school matter at any time. The Secretary of State can assign other school related functions to HMCI, including the training of teachers (but not the training of the whole school workforce: see part 3, page 51). HMCI has to have regard to 'government policy' as the Secretary of State may direct.

## Section 3: annual and other reports to the Secretary of State

HMCI is required to make an annual written report to the Secretary of State, who in turn must lay this report before Parliament. HMCI has the authority to publish any report made by him under this section in whatever manner he sees fit (this remains the same as in SIA s. 2(7)).

## Section 4: powers of entry, etc. for the purposes of section 2

HMCI has a right of entry to any school in England, and to other premises related to the education of pupils, for example key stage 4 work-place learning, in order to undertake the duties placed on HMCI under s. 2 (see above). It includes the right to inspect and take copies of relevant documentation. It is an offence intentionally to obstruct HMCI and section 4(4) specifies the penalty for this offence, namely a fine not exceeding level 4 on the standard scale (at June 2005 the maximum fine is £2500). By virtue of schedule 1(5), the right of entry extends to HMI, other members of HMCI's staff and additional inspectors, but only those empowered to lead inspections (see s.1 above).

# Inspections

Sections 5 to 10 are the heart of the new school inspection system. Section 5 replaces the statutory basis of the current 'section 10' (of the SIA 1996) inspections. It contains the duty to inspect, and specifies what should be inspected and which schools should be inspected.

It is worth noting that Ofsted's *Framework for Inspecting Schools* has no specific statutory basis. This is unlike the Framework for Inspection of Children's Services under s. 21 of the Children Act 2004. The latter framework requires the consent of the Secretary of State. The new 'section 5' inspections will begin in September 2005 and, at the time of writing (June 2005), drafts (9 March 2005) of the *Framework* and associated documents can be found at www.ofsted.gov.uk/publications/index.cfm?fuseaction=pubs.summary&id=3861 and draft *Regulations* (2 June 2005), which prescribe intervals between inspections, etc. could be found at www.dfes.gov.uk/consultations/conDetails.cfm?consultationId=1348.

Section 6 ensures that parents are notified of an inspection but they are no longer invited to a meeting. Section 7 requires HMCI to take account of any views expressed by a range of partners. Section 8 allows HMCI to inspect a school when not required either by the Secretary of State or the 'section 5' inspection arrangements. Section 9 allows HMCI to deem such an inspection to be a 'section 5' inspection. Section 10 defines HMCI powers of entry.

## Section 5: duty to inspect certain schools at prescribed intervals

Section 5(1) places a duty on HMCI to inspect and report on the schools in England at prescribed intervals; the draft School Inspection Regulations require HMCI to inspect every school by 1 August 2009 and thereafter inspect schools within 3 years from the end of the school year in which the last inspection of that school took place (which could mean that occasionally there is nearly 4 years between inspections). Section 5(1) differs from the previous position (s.10(1) of the SIA) in that HMCI was required to secure that schools were inspected by registered inspectors. The requirement to have a lay inspector is also removed.

The definition of which schools are to be inspected remains the same as in the SIA: all LEA-maintained schools (community, foundation, voluntary, special and nursery) and certain schools in the independent sector that are mainly state funded, namely academies, city technology colleges (CTCs) and non-maintained special schools approved by the Secretary of State under s. 342 of the Education Act 1996. By virtue of schedule 1(5),

HMCI can delegate inspection work to HMI, other members of HMCI's staff and additional inspectors who are authorised to lead inspections. As in the SIA, HMCI has discretion not to inspect a closing school (s.5(3) and (4)).

Section 5(5) requires inspection reports to cover the same four areas currently covered by reports under s.10(5) of SIA 1996 (which mirror HMCI's reporting duties) with the addition of how far the education provided meets the needs of the range of pupils and of the contribution made by the school to the well-being of its pupils. (See commentary on section 2 above on HMCI's general duty on keeping the Secretary of State informed for further information and definitions.) The two additional areas that were added by amendments in the House of Lords (namely HMCI's duty to keep the Secretary of State informed on the development of self-evaluation, and behaviour and attendance) are not required to be covered in school inspections.

Section 5(6) is a technical provision referring to s. 9, which enables HMCI to deem that an inspection for another purpose can be a 'section 5' inspection. Section 5(7) excludes denominational education and relevant collective worship in voluntary and foundation schools with a religious character from 'section 5' inspections. Such educational provision is to be inspected under s. 48.

## Section 6: duty to notify parents of section 5 inspection

The new inspection arrangements repeal the requirement (schedule 6(3) of the SIA 1996) that schools arrange a meeting between parents and the inspectors. This is not re-enacted because of the very short notice of inspections in the new system. This was of great concern to members of the House of Lords. On 10 February 2005, the then Parliamentary Secretary (Lord Filkin) at the DfES wrote to Baroness Sharp that:

*Ofsted has had concerns about the effectiveness of the present statutory meeting in securing the involvement of parents in the inspection process. […] Ofsted continues to trial new and innovative ways of involving parents in the inspection, many of which have been welcomed by parents. These include the following mechanisms:*

- *A questionnaire to be added to* [the] *letter that parents receive from the school notifying them of the inspection. The letter will include contact details for the lead inspector so that parents can speak to inspectors directly. The letter and questionnaire will also be translated into community languages.*

- *During inspections, requesting that schools pin a notice to the door of the main entrance to let parents know that the inspection is taking place.*

- *Holding a one-hour meeting with parents at the end of the school day for those parents who are available.*

- *Giving parents' views more prominence in inspection reports as a lever to encourage schools to take more responsibility for gathering parents' views.*

- *Sharing best practice would help schools in gathering parents' views, for example encouraging parent governors to set up focus groups to gather views at regular intervals and summarise these for the inspection.*

As a result of pressure from Peers, section 6(2) was added to the Bill by way of a Government amendment: the appropriate authority (see comment on s. 6(3) below) is required, using a statement prepared by HMCI, to invite parents to give their views on the school.

Section 6(3) defines the 'appropriate authority' for a 'section 5' inspection as the governing body of an LEA-maintained school, but it is the LEA if the school does not have a delegated budget. The 'appropriate authority' for independent schools that have 'section 5' inspections is the 'proprietor'.

The 'appropriate authority', when notified by HMCI that a 'section 5' inspection will take place must take reasonable steps to inform the parents and other prescribed persons (s. 6(1)). The draft *School Inspection Regulations* require LEA-maintained school governing bodies to inform 'a person appearing to them to be an appropriate officer of the LEA' (presumably a formulation to overcome the progressive replacement of the statutory chief education officer post by a director of children's services during the period up to April 2008), and LEAs to inform the chair of governors where the school does not have a delegated budget. For voluntary schools, the person who appoints foundation governors has to be informed, and for voluntary aided schools the 'appropriate diocesan authority' also has to be informed. In addition, independent special schools must inform any local authority that is paying fees for a pupil at the school, and all schools must inform an appropriate officer of the local authority for every looked-after child at the school. The Learning and Skills Council (LSC) must be informed for secondary schools whether or not the school has post-16 provision.

## Section 7: duty to have regard to views of certain persons

HMCI must have regard to the views of the headteacher, the governing body or proprietor, staff, pupils, parents and any persons notified of the inspection, where those views are expressed. This section was added after Opposition pressure in the House of

Lords and is innovative in that it expressly requires inspectors to take account of the views of pupils.

### Section 8: inspection at discretion of the Chief Inspector

As before (s. 3(1) of SIA 1996) HMCI has an absolute discretion to inspect any school even though a 'section 5' inspection is not required and the Secretary of State has not asked for one. The *Explanatory Notes* (DfES, 2005b) state that this provision 'enables the Chief Inspector to conduct inspections for a range of purposes, including monitoring visits by HMI to schools in special measures, visits to schools to aid him in keeping the Secretary of State informed under section 2, or to contribute to reports on, for example, the teaching in a single curriculum subject'.

### Section 9: power of the Chief Inspector to treat discretionary inspection as section 5 inspection

HMCI is able to treat an inspection conducted under his/her own power (s. 8) or at the request of the Secretary of State (s. 2(2)(b)) as though it were a 'section 5' inspection. This will enable a school that is inspected under s. 8 or s. 2(2)(b) to avoid having to have a 'section 5' inspection under the normal timetable as well. However, if the inspection is deemed to be a 'section 5' inspection then the chapter 2 requirements on reporting to parents will apply, as will HMCI's power to find that the school is causing concern. (See sections 13 and 14 on pages 17 and 18.)

### Section 10: power of entry, etc. for purposes of inspection under sections 5 or 8

HMCI is given the same rights of entry for 'section 5' and 'section 8' inspections as for 'section 2' inspections (see notes on s. 4 above). The same offence is created for those obstructing an inspection. This replaces s. 3(3) and schedule 3(7) of the SIA 1996 without substantive change.

## Publication of inspection reports

### Section 11: publication of inspection reports

HMCI can publish any school inspection report by any appropriate means including, for example, electronic publication on the Ofsted website. The draft *Framework for Inspecting*

*Schools* (Ofsted, 2005a) states that inspection reports will be published within three calendar weeks of the conclusion of the inspection (para. 47). Section 11(3) gives HMCI legal protection for the purposes of the law of defamation in any report unless malice can be shown. This enables inspection findings to be protected from aggrieved school staff suing for libel, etc.

## Section 12: interpretation of chapter 1

Section 12 contains statutory definitions. The definition of 'well-being' is referred to in the comment on s. 2 (see earlier).

# Chapter 2: procedure for inspections under chapter 1

This chapter sets out what schools have to do with inspection reports and what happens when a school is judged to be causing concern. Section 13 gives HMCI's functions in relation to schools causing concern. Sections 14 (LEA-maintained schools) and 16 (independent schools) state what should happen to reports, and sections 15 (LEA-maintained schools) and 17 (independent schools) state what action the school and/or the LEA must take when a school causes concern.

There are new definitions for schools causing concern (see chapter 5, sections 44 to 46 below).

# Inspections and reports: all schools

## Section 13: duties of Chief Inspector where a school causes or has caused concern

Section 13 covers the circumstances in which a 'section 5' inspection has found that a school requires either special measures or significant improvement and also deals with cases where such a designation is already in place and a judgement is required to change or removed it. The section re-enacts and changes previous legislation (ss. 14 and 16A of SIA 1996). The provisions of this section also link to the requirement that an HMI, specifically authorised by HMCI, must confirm the inspector's finding that the school is causing concern (see commentary on schedule 1(5)(3) earlier).

If a school is found to be causing concern, that is if the school requires either 'special measures' or 'significant improvement', HMCI must follow certain procedures. Firstly, a draft of the report must be sent to the governing body (or proprietor for an independent school) (s. 13(2)(a)); but pressure in the House of Lords led to the addition of s. 13(2)(b), which requires HMCI to consider any comments within a prescribed period, defined as five working days in the draft *School Inspection Regulations*. Section 13(3) requires HMCI to inform the Secretary of State, the LEA (for maintained schools only) and the governing body/proprietor that the school requires special measures or significant improvement.

Section 13(4) deals with the case where a school was designated as 'requiring special measures' in a previous inspection report. If HMCI is now of the opinion that the school no longer requires special measures then the report must state this opinion. If HMCI considers a designation of 'requiring significant improvement' rather than special measures is appropriate, this must be stated in the report. Section 13(5) deals with the case of a school already designated as 'requiring significant improvement'. If HMCI is of the opinion that a school does not require special measures or significant improvement, this must be stated in the report. If such a school now requires special measures then the procedure in s.13(1) will commence.

# Destination of reports and measures required: maintained schools

## Section 14: destination of reports: maintained schools

HMCI must send the report of a 'section 5' inspection without delay to the governing body, the LEA, the headteacher, and the body or bodies that appoint foundation governors. The Secretary of State can prescribe other bodies that should receive the report, although none are mentioned in the draft School Inspection Regulations (s. 14(1) and (2)). A report must be sent to the Learning and Skills Council if the school provides post-compulsory school education (s. 14(3)). The governing body (or LEA if the LEA has withdrawn delegation) must make the report available for public inspection at reasonable times, provide a copy of the report free of charge to anyone who asks (but may charge a fee not exceeding the cost of supply), and send a copy to every parent of a child at the school within a prescribed period (defined as five working days in the draft *School Inspection Regulations*) (s. 14(4)). The main difference from s. 16 of the SIA 1996 is that a summary of the report no longer has to be produced and sent to parents. The new style reports, in keeping with the shorter inspection, will be limited to approximately 6 to 12 pages. See www.ofsted.gov.uk/publications/index.cfm?fuseaction=pubs.displayfile&id=3854&type=pdf for a draft template of the new report, which includes a two-page summary for students/pupils at the school.

## Section 15: measures to be taken by the local education authority

Section 15 applies where a school is found to be a cause for concern after an inspection (see s. 44 for definitions of a school that requires special measures or a significant improvement). It replaces ss. 17 and 18 of SIA 1996, which required every school to produce an action plan whether the school was causing concern or not, and required the LEA to prepare an action plan where the school required special measures. It should be noted that the LEA was not under a duty to prepare an action plan where the school was found to have serious weaknesses, an inadequate sixth form or be underachieving, although invariably LEAs did produce plans for such schools. Under the 2005 Act only the LEA has to produce an action plan, called a 'written statement of any action', and only in the case of a school causing concern. The action plan no longer has to be sent to the Secretary of State, although interestingly the Secretary of State can direct that a plan must be produced in a shorter period so in those circumstances it is to be expected that the Secretary of State would wish to see it. The holder of that office has sufficient general powers to require such information to be submitted without it being specified here.

The LEA is under a duty to prepare an action plan for a school found to be causing concern after a 'section 5' inspection. The plan must state the action that the LEA proposes to take and the timetable for this action. Where the LEA proposes to take no action in response to the inspection report, the statement must set out their reasons for not taking action. A copy of the plan must be sent to HMCI and, in the case of voluntary-aided schools, to the bodies who appoint foundation governors (if any) and the diocesan authorities for Church of England and Roman Catholic Schools (s. 15(2)). The deadline for the production of the action plan will be prescribed in regulations; the draft *School Inspection Regulations* state that this will be 10 working days from the publication of the inspection report, but the Secretary of State may require a shorter period in urgent cases (s. 15(3)).

# Destination of reports and measures required: non-maintained schools

## Section 16: destination of reports: non-maintained schools

Section 16 re-enacts s. 20 of the SIA 1996 with modifications. It is similar to s. 14 (see above) but applies to the independent schools which are subject to 'section 5' inspections, that is: academies, CTCs and non-maintained special schools. Unlike s. 14 though, HMCI is not under a duty to send the report to the LSC or the LEA in which the school is situated. HMCI must send the report to the school proprietor, which in most cases will be the 'governing body' (s. 16(1)), and the proprietor must make the report available for inspection at the school, provide a copy to anyone who wants one and make arrangements for parents to receive a copy (s. 16(3)). Section 16(2) places a duty on the proprietor of a non-maintained special school to send a copy of the report to any LEA that is paying fees for pupils at that school.

### Section 17: statement to be prepared by proprietor of school

Section 17 updates s. 21 of SIA 1996. If a 'section 5' inspection report states that the independent school requires special measures or significant improvement, the proprietor is required to prepare an action plan and a timetable for its implementation (s. 17(1)). The deadline for the production of the action plan will be prescribed in regulations; the draft *School Inspection Regulations* state that this will be 10 working days from the publication of the inspection report, but the Secretary of State may require a shorter period in urgent cases (s. 17(2)). A copy of the plan must be sent to HMCI and prescribed persons, although it is clear from the draft *School Inspection Regulations* that the Secretary of State is not proposing to use this power immediately. In the case of a non-maintained special school, the action plan must be sent to any LEA that is paying fees for a pupil at the school (s. 17(4)).

### Section 18: interpretation of chapter 2

Statutory definitions are already covered in ss. 13 to 17 above.

## Chapters 3 and 4

Chapter 3 School Inspectors and School Inspections: Wales and chapter 4 Procedure for Inspections under Chapter 3 (ss. 19 to 43, and schedules 2 to 4) apply exclusively to Wales.

## Chapter 5: schools causing concern

Currently, there are four categories of schools causing concern following an Ofsted inspection.

- The finding of a 'school requiring special measures' was introduced with the original Ofsted legislation in 1992 and is found in s. 13(9) of the SIA 1996. A school is defined as requiring special measures 'if the school is failing, or likely to fail, to give its pupils an acceptable standard of education'.

- The 'serious weakness' category is defined in s. 15(5) of the School Standards and Framework Act (SSFA) 1998 as a school 'although giving its pupils in general an acceptable standard of education … has significant weaknesses in one or more areas of its activities'.

- The 'inadequate sixth form' is defined in schedule 7(1)(2) of the Learning and Skills Act 2000 as '(a) the school is failing or likely to fail to give pupils over compulsory school-age an acceptable standard of education, or (b) the school has significant weaknesses in one or more areas of its activities for pupils over compulsory school age'.

- The 'underachieving' category is defined in DfES guidance, *Schools Causing Concern* (DfES, 2002) as 'schools identified via Ofsted inspection as schools where pupils are not achieving as well as they could and should, and which are themselves not achieving as well as schools in similar situations'.

Section 44 defines the two new categories of schools causing concern, and ss. 45 and 46, and schedule 5, make minor and technical changes, including updating statutory references. Further minor changes are made by schedule 9.

## Section 44: categories of schools causing concern

Two statutory categories of schools causing concern are defined in s. 44: those that require special measures and those that require significant improvement.

Section 44(1) states that special measures are required if:

a) the school is failing to give its pupils an acceptable standard of education, and

b) the persons responsible for leading, managing or governing the school are not demonstrating the capacity to secure the necessary improvement in the school.

There are two changes in this definition:

- paragraph (b) requires inspectors to take into account the school's capacity to improve, and

- the 'likely to fail' judgment is removed. That is, schools will no longer be regarded as requiring special measures merely because the inspector thinks they will or may deteriorate.

The reason for this change was explained by the then Parliamentary Secretary at the Wales Office, Don Touhig MP, in Committee as follows.

*Occasionally, schools have been placed in special measures because they are not providing an acceptable standard of education despite having acquired the capacity to*

*improve. That may have resulted, for example, from a recent change of leadership that is demonstrably driving the school forward. The school may already have made an accurate self-evaluation of its provision that coincides with the inspection findings, and it may already be well on the way to putting things right. It is not difficult to imagine the frustration likely to be felt by a strong head teacher if the school is then placed in special measures. That could knock the school back. The progress that it was making could be halted by the adverse effect on staff morale of a special measures judgment in such circumstances. The Government's view is that it makes no sense to place in special measures a school that is already well on the way to recovery.*
(Hansard, Standing Committee A, 22 March 2005, cols 24 and 35.)

The Minister also explained that a school that is 'likely to fail' (using the SIA 1996 definition) would be caught by the new definition of 'requiring significant improvement'.

Section 44(2) introduces the new category of a school 'requiring significant improvement', which is defined as a school not requiring special measures but as one 'performing significantly less well than it might in all the circumstances reasonably be expected to perform'.

The *Explanatory Notes* state that the existing categories of serious weaknesses, inadequate sixth forms, and underachieving are expected to fall into this new category.

## Section 45: cases where the Secretary of State or Assembly may direct closure of school

The SSFA 1998 introduced the 'serious weakness' category in order to enable LEAs and the Secretary of State to take action against a school falling within this category. Section 19 of the SSFA 1998, as amended by s. 56 of the Education Act 2002, gives the Secretary of State power to direct an LEA to close a school that either has serious weaknesses or requires special measures. Section 45 (of the 2005 Act) amends section 19 to restrict this power to apply only to schools that require special measures.

In all other cases, the requiring 'significant improvement' category is substituted for the 'serious weaknesses' category. These amendments are found in paras 14 to 20 of schedule 9 (further amendments relating to school inspection) to the 2005 Act covering sections 14 to 18A of the SSFA. The effect is to enable these powers to be used to support schools that at present fall into the 'underachieving' category as in future they will require 'significant improvement'. Thus, the LEA will be able to appoint additional governors to 'underachieving schools' under the amended s. 18 of the SSFA.

## Section 46 and schedule 5: sixth forms requiring significant improvement

Section 46 adds schedule 5 to the Act. The Learning and Skills Act 2000 introduced the category of an 'inadequate sixth form' and schedule 7 of that Act is extensively amended. The new definition of a 'sixth form requiring significant improvement' now appears in para. 3(3) of schedule 5 to the 2005 Act, which replaces para. 1(2) of schedule 7 to the 2000 Act. A school requires significant improvement in relation to its sixth form if:

a) the school is failing to give its pupils over compulsory school age an acceptable standard of education

b) in relation to its provision for pupils over compulsory school age, the school is performing significantly less well than it might in all the circumstances reasonably be expected to perform.

The definition contains elements of the 'requiring special measures' category in (a) and the requiring 'significant improvement' category in (b). The remaining amendments to schedule 7 of the 2000 Act are mainly updating statutory references including references to area inspections of 14 to19 provision under s. 65 of the 2000 Act. Two findings of a 'sixth form requiring significant improvement' are required to trigger the LSC review procedure in parts 2 and 3 of schedule 7. This can result in the sixth form being closed.

# Chapter 6: other inspections: England and Wales: inspection of religious education

Voluntary and foundation schools may have a religious character. These schools are usually referred to as faith schools and, where permitted, will have religious education and collective worship distinctive of the religion or religious denomination that established the school. Separate inspection arrangements are provided for this aspect of relevant schools in ss. 47 to 50 and schedule 6; although only ss. 47 to 49 apply to England.

In debate in the House of Lords, the then DfES Parliamentary Secretary, Lord Filkin, stated that it was intended to make these inspections as 'congruous' as possible with the 'section 5' inspections. Lord Filkin said, 'We do not want to see schools subjected to multiple inspections' and announced that a protocol was being discussed to allow information sharing on a confidential basis in order to enable inspections to take place together (Lords Hansard, 13 January 2005, col. 451).

## Section 47: meaning of 'denominational education'

Section 47 defines that schools will have denominational education inspected under s. 48, that is religious education in accordance with the religious character of the school. These will mainly be voluntary-aided schools, the vast majority of which are supported by the Roman Catholic or Anglican Churches. There are, of course, a smaller number of schools adhering to other Christian denominations and a growing number attached to other faiths. Most religious education in a foundation or voluntary-controlled school will be in accordance with the religious education agreed syllabus and therefore inspected by a 'section 5' inspection, but any that is provided in accordance with the school's religious character will need a 'section 48' inspection.

The new 'section 48' inspections do not apply to faith-based CTCs or academies, although Lord Filkin said, 'the same objective can be achieved by stipulating them [inspections of denomination education and collective worship] in the funding agreement for each academy and CTC' that has a religious character (Lords Hansard, 13 January 2005, col. 451).

## Section 48: inspection of religious education: England

The governing body of a voluntary or foundation school with a religious character is under a duty to ensure that denominational education and collective worship are inspected (s. 48(1)). For a voluntary-controlled school, the foundation governors decide, and for a foundation or voluntary-aided school, the whole governing body decides, who is to conduct the inspection. An innovation over the current 'section 23' inspections of the SIA 1996 is that there must be prior consultation with a prescribed body about who is to conduct the inspection (s. 48(2)). This is to ensure that the inspector is sufficiently 'rigorous to identify areas for improvement in the teaching of the faith' (Lord Filkin, Lords Hansard, 13 January 2005, col. 450). The prescribed bodies are set out in the draft *School Inspection Regulations* and include the diocesan authorities for Church of England and Roman Catholic schools, and the Jewish Studies Education Inspection Service for Jewish schools. Section 48(3) enables the interval between inspections to be prescribed; the draft *Regulations* state three years. (But see section 5(1) above.) The inspection must report on the quality of denominational education and the content of collective worship, and may report on the spiritual, moral, social and cultural development of pupils (s. 48(4)). The inspector may use assistants to help with the inspection provided they are 'fit and proper' persons (s. 48(5)).

### Section 49: procedure for inspections under section 48

This section re-enacts procedures currently covered by schedule 4 to SIA 1996. The Secretary of State can prescribe in regulations the period within which an inspection under s. 48 may be conducted, and the draft *Regulations* state a period of 10 days (s. 49(1)). The person conducting the inspection has to prepare a report in writing before the end of a prescribed period, which the draft regulations state is within 15 days of the end of the inspection (s. 49(2)). The inspector must then send the report to the governing body (s. 49(3)) and the governing body must make the report available to members of the public and ensure that all parents of registered pupils receive a copy of the report.

### Section 50 and schedule 6: inspection of religious education: Wales

This section and schedule apply exclusively to Wales.

## Chapter 6: other inspections: England and Wales: LEA inspections

### Section 51: power of the LEA to inspect a maintained school for a specific purpose

The existing power that LEAs have to inspect provision in schools that they maintain under s. 25 of SIA 1996 is re-enacted in s. 51. The inspection must be to collect information about any matter in connection with the LEA's functions and that cannot be obtained reasonably practically in any other way (s. 51(1)). An LEA officer has a right of entry to collect information at all reasonable times (s. 51(2)).

### Section 52: provision of inspection services by LEAs in Wales

Section 52 re-enacts the current s. 24 of the SIA for Wales alone. As a consequence, the power that LEAs in England had to provide a 'section 10' inspection service is repealed. Arguably, local authorities could use powers under the Local Government Act 2003 to provide such a service, although given the size of the contracts for the new inspection arrangements, it is very unlikely that an LEA would be able to tender successfully.

# Chapter 6: other inspections: England and Wales: inspection of child minding, day care and nursery education

## Section 53 and schedule 7: inspection of child minding, day care and nursery education

Section 53 adds schedule 7 to the Act and revises Ofsted's functions for the inspection of childminding and day care (part 1 of the schedule), and nursery education (part 2). Ofsted acquired the role of registering and inspecting childminding and day care from local government in 2001 following the Care Standards Act 2000. The original legislation is found in sections 79N to 79R and s. 79U of the Children Act 1989. Ofsted acquired the role of inspecting relevant nursery education in 1996 and the legislation was revised in the SSFA 1998 and is found in s. 122 and schedule 26 of that Act. It applies to nursery education that is funded through local government and the early years development and childcare partnerships. Nursery education provided at LEA-maintained primary and nursery schools will continue to be inspected under s. 5 of the 2005 Act.

The two inspection regimes use 'registered inspectors'. The nursery education inspectorate started as mainly independent contractors similar to the school registered inspectors but the initial core of the inspectors for childminding and day care were transferred from local authority employment. The statutory basis of both inspectorates is located in schedule 26 of the SSFA 1998. Virtually all inspectors are now Ofsted employees and many staff are able to inspect all three elements of child minding, day care and nursery education. Schedule 7 (of the 2005 Act) removes the register of inspectors (in England), revises the law on what should be reported on in an inspection, makes a few other minor changes and updates statutory references.

All the references below to paras are to paras of schedule 7. Several details will be prescribed in regulations made by the Secretary of State. The DfES published draft *Regulations* on 1 April 2005; at the time of writing the draft could be found at www.dfes.gov.uk/consultations/conDetails.cfm?consultationId=1305.

### Child minding and day care

HMCI's general duty to keep the Secretary of State informed about child minding and day care provided in England is expanded in para. 1. Currently, HMCI has a duty to report on the quality and standards of child minding and day care. In addition, HMCI must now report on:

- how far child minding and day care meet the needs of the range of children cared for
- the contribution made by child minding and day care to the well-being of the children for whom they are provided
- the quality of the leadership and management of day care.

See section 2 (page 10) for the equivalent duty on HMCI in respect of schools. Well-being is defined similarly in accordance with s. 10(2) of the Children Act 2004.

Paragraph 2 removes HMCI's duty to maintain a register of early years child care inspectors in England and para. 3 gives HMCI a duty to arrange inspections, which was formerly done by registered inspectors. A new duty is placed on the provider of the provision to notify prescribed persons of the inspection. The draft *Regulations* state this will include parents must be notified but this duty does not apply to crèches or open access provision. HMCI acquires an extended duty on what has to be covered by each inspection, which reflects the reporting duty to the Secretary of State (see notes on para. 1 above.)

Paragraph 4 requires HMCI to produce and distribute inspection reports. A copy must go to the day care provider or child minder. Regulations can prescribe other people or authorities who should receive a report and the draft regulations prescribe the local authority for the area in which the provision is situated. Day care providers and child minders must provide a copy of the report to prescribed persons. The draft regulations prescribe that parents of children must receive a report within 30 days of the inspection. HMCI can publish the report electronically. Paragraph 6 applies the rights of entry for school inspectors to the inspectors of day care and child minding. (See section 10 on page 16.)

### Nursery education

Paragraph 7 amends s. 122 of the SSFA 1998 to remove HMCI's responsibility to maintain a register of nursery inspectors in England. Paragraph 9 rectifies an anomaly arising from the hasty removal, under the Children Act 2004, of the duty to have an early years and childcare development plan. The reference to the plan is removed and replaced by an LEA duty to secure sufficient provision of nursery education.

HMCI's general duty to keep the Secretary of State informed is expanded in para. 11. Currently, HMCI has to report on the quality and standards of nursery education, and the spiritual, moral, social and cultural development of the children for whom nursery education is provided. HMCI will now have to report on:

- how far relevant nursery education meets the needs of the range of children for whom it is provided

- the contribution made by relevant nursery education to the well-being of the children for whom it is provided

- the quality of the leadership and management of nursery education.

This is similar to HMCI's duty for child minding and day care (see comments on para. 1 on page 27). The term 'well-being' is defined in para. 10 in accordance with s. 10(2) of the Children Act 2004. (See section 2 on page 16.)

HMCI's duty to maintain a register of inspectors is removed in paras 13 to 19, mainly by making the existing legislation apply only to Wales, and replacing it for England with a duty to inspect nursery education, inserted as new paragraph 6B of the schedule 26 of the SSFA 1998 (para. 12). HMCI must inspect provision at prescribed intervals, and inspect provision 'under consideration for funding', that is private and voluntary-sector provision seeking public funding in the form of grant aid. HMCI can also inspect provision at any other time that he/she considers appropriate. The previous reference to inspecting provision 'at any premises' of the provider is removed, enabling the inspection to take place without having to visit every set of premises managed by the provider. The duty does not apply to nursery education provided by a school, which will receive a 'section 5' inspection.

A new regulation-making power is inserted to require the 'responsible person' (see below) to notify prescribed persons that an inspection is to take place. The draft regulations prescribe the interval for inspection as three years, and make it clear that the responsible person is the proprietor, person in charge of local authority-funded provision, etc., and the parents of children using the provision are people who must be informed about the inspection. Paragraph 12 also inserts a new paragraph 6B into schedule 26, setting out the issues that HMCI must inspect in each nursery education setting. This reflects the duty to report to the Secretary of State (see note on para. 11 above).

HMCI is responsible for the production and distribution of all reports (para. 20). A copy must go to the nursery's 'responsible person'. Regulations can prescribe other people or authorities who should receive a report. The draft regulations require the 'responsible person' to provide a copy of the report to the local authority for the area in which the provision is situated, and that parents of children must receive a copy of the report within 30 days of inspection. HMCI can publish the report electronically.

The annual report of HMCI (see s. 3 above) has to include an account of HMCI's work on inspecting nursery education (para. 21). HMCI's rights of access to conduct inspections is found in para. 24(3).

# Chapter 6: other inspections: England and Wales: inspection of independent schools

## Section 54 and schedule 8: amendments relating to inspection of independent schools

The Education Act 2002 introduced a new inspection regime for schools in the independent sector other than those that will receive a 'section 5' inspection. Amendments to the 2002 Act (in schedule 8 of the 2005 Act) are needed because of the removal of 'registered inspectors' in England. Provision for inspections in England and Wales is separated, with the England inspections found in para. 2 (inserting new sections 162A and 162B into the 2002 Act) and the Wales inspections in para. 3 (new sections 163 and 164 in the 2002 Act). There are no changes to HMCI's powers to have a school in the independent sector inspected, which derive from the requirement for independent schools to register with the DfES and for the 'registration authority' to require HMCI to inspect. Inspection is against expected standards (prescribed in regulations) with similar powers to enter premises and gather information that exist for the maintained sector. HMCI has an additional power to levy fees from independent schools that are inspected.

## Sections 55 to 57: inspection of careers services in Wales, etc.

These sections relate exclusively to Wales.

# Chapter 7: supplementary

## Section 58: inspection of computer records

Section 58 re-enacts section 42 of SIA 1996 without change. Any person engaged in inspection work is entitled to inspect the operation of any computer on which records and documents are held, and to require whoever operates the computer system to assist in any inspection. This will enable Ofsted inspectors to check a school's computer records as part of a school inspection. Paragraphs 13 and 26 of schedule 9 apply s. 58 to the inspection of LEA and Connexions Services.

## Section 59: combined reports

Section 59 allows Ofsted to produce a single report that combines the inspection findings of school-aged and early-years provision at the same establishment, for example where an independent school secures funded nursery education in the same building or a maintained school arranges day care as part of its extended school provision.

An inspection carried out under two or more of the following provisions can be produced as a single report (s. 59(1) and (2)):

- part 1 of the 2005 Act, that is s. 2 or s. 5 inspections, etc.
- part 10A of the Children Act 1989, that is inspections of child minding and day care
- s. 122 and schedule 26 of the SSFA 1998, that is inspection of nursery education
- chapter 1 of part 10 of the Education Act 2002, that is inspection of independent schools.

Interestingly, the report of LEA-funded and secured youth service provision under the management of a school could not be included in a 'section 5' inspection report as the statutory basis for inspecting the youth service provision lies in s. 38 of the Education Act 1997.

Section 59(3) to (5) make additional provision for combined reports. Any legal requirements on the publication and distribution of inspection findings in a combined report apply to any other inspection reported on in the combined report. HMCI can publish combined reports in any appropriate manner, but this does not override any duties as to publication in other legislation, for example a combined report that includes a 'section 5' inspection and inspection of day care must be given to parents of children attending the school or the day care.

## Section 60: repeal of School Inspections Act 1996

The whole of the School Inspections Act 1996 is repealed.

## Section 61 and schedule 9: further amendments relating to school inspection

Section 61 adds schedule 9 to the Act, making consequential amendments to other legislation. Most are of little or no consequence, for example updating the statutory reference to ensure that HMCI is disbarred from being a Member of the House of Commons. The consequential amendments to the SSFA 1998 for schools causing concern have been mentioned under s. 45 above. Paragraph 11 of schedule 9 updates the reference to the use of additional inspectors for LEA inspections under the 1997 Education Act. HMCI will be under a duty to publish the qualifications and experience of non-HMI conducting these inspections, and if HMCI enters into an agreement with an 'inspection service provider' to provide additional inspectors for LEA inspections, the names of these additional inspectors must be published.

## Section 62: power of the Assembly to change inspection framework for Wales

Applies exclusively to Wales. The Welsh Assembly is empowered to change the school inspection arrangements in Wales to those that will prevail in England without recourse to a further Act of Parliament.

## Section 63: interpretation of part 1

This section contains statutory definitions.

# Part 2  School organisation

## Introduction

The law on school organisation is about how schools are created, changed and closed, and who can make proposals to change schools. School organisation law covers not just the size and age range of schools but whether they are single-sex or mixed, have boarding provision and the category: community, voluntary or foundation and whether, for the latter two categories, the school has, or has not, a religious character. The SSFA 1998 rewrote the law on school organisation. Subsequent Acts have amended the law, and the Education Act 2005 makes further amendments.

## Competitions for secondary schools

The main change in the 2005 Act is on competitions for secondary schools. The Education Act 2002 established the principle of competitions for new secondary schools but only where, according to s. 70(7), an 'additional' secondary school was required, that is one that does not replace a 'discontinued' school. The DfES statutory guidance made it clear that a new school that caters for a growth in pupil numbers would be subject to competition but a school established by the amalgamation of two or more existing schools, i.e. a 'replacement', would not. Similarly, a new school is not an additional school if an existing school is transferring to a new site or if its premises are being rebuilt. (*Secretary of State guidance for decision makers on statutory proposals for changes in school organisation*, section 3, paragraphs 2 to 4).

The new law was introduced in June 2003 and there had been no competitions up to February 2005 (Written Parliamentary Answer, 28 February 2005). However, a BBC report of 10 November 2003 stated that the London borough of Lambeth had organised a competition and several newspapers reported in April 2005 that a parent group is promoting Elmcourt Secondary School as a voluntary-controlled school in the borough.

The Government's view as to why there were no competitions is summed up in the *Regulatory Impact Assessment* to the Bill which states that:

> *LEAs have mainly avoided the requirement to have a competition either through starting their consultation before the regulations came into effect, by reaching agreements with individual promoters of foundation or voluntary-aided schools or by entering into agreements with sponsors to establish academies instead of holding competitions.*

In 2003 there were nine replacement secondary schools, seven in 2004 and none to date in 2005 (Lords Written Parliamentary Answer, 4 February 2005). These include schools formed out of reorganisations and amalgamations and also schools with a religious character replacing existing community schools. However, the RIA estimates that there will be 20 competitions each year in future at a cost of £25,000 per competition. Three days of free DfES consultancy will be offered to help any new group develop proposals for competitions (pp. 58 and 59).

## Five Year Strategy and competitions for new secondary schools

The DfES *Five Year Strategy for Children and Learners* (DfES, 2004a) contains several proposals for changes in school organisation. Two of these, namely providing a fast-track procedure for community and voluntary-controlled secondary schools to acquire foundation status and the expansion of popular and successful secondary schools, did not require an Act of Parliament.

The Five Year Strategy states that:

> *We will mandate competitions for new schools where they are needed, so that it* [is] *easier for new promoters – including parents' groups – to open schools in response to local demand.*
> (page 52, paragraph 38)

On the publication day of the *Five Year Strategy* (8 July 2004), the DfES wrote to national organisations about the proposed changes to school organisation legislation. The DfES confirmed the intention to extend the requirement for competitions for new secondary schools from additional secondary schools only to all circumstances where proposals for new secondary schools need to be published. Another proposal in the DfES letter, that the legislation should give foundation bodies the power to publish proposals to establish schools, including entering into a competition for a new secondary school, is not in the Act. This proposal was not taken forward as the DfES concluded existing legislation was sufficient. See DfES letter of 7 January 2005 from Stephen Crowne (a DfES official) headed *4th Session Education Bill: School Organisation and Restriction on the Disposal of Land*.

## Government policy on new secondary schools

Two quotations will help to set the Government's policy context for the change. Stephen Crowne's letter (mentioned above) states that the legislation is:

*...consistent with the modernised role for local authorities as commissioners of educa-*
*tion, rather than direct providers, set out in the Five Year Strategy. [The legislation is]*
*intended to give local people a greater say over the establishment of secondary*
*schools in their areas. Local people will have more opportunities to come up with their*
*own proposals to establish schools; and they will be able to make their views known*
*on a range of options, rather than on a single option put forward by the local authori-*
*ty or an individual promoter.*

*Local authorities will retain their strategic planning role. It will accordingly be for*
*local authorities to determine the need for new secondary schools and the key charac-*
*teristics of schools in terms, for example, of their location, the number of places*
*needed and age range. Promoters will be invited to bring forward proposals for*
*schools on the basis of a specification drawn up by the local authority; and of course*
*the local authorities would also be free to publish their own proposals on the same*
*basis. As a general rule, local authorities inviting proposals will be expected to take*
*responsibility for bearing the cost of providing new school buildings, regardless of*
*who the promoters are of the successful proposals. In many cases, new secondary*
*schools are likely to be established as part of wider reorganisations undertaken*
*through BSF* [Building Schools for the Future programme].

The Government's approach to improving secondary education and the BSF capital programme (to replace or modernise every secondary school over a 15-year period) was set
out in the Commons Committee debate by the then Parliamentary Secretary at the DfES,
Derek Twigg on 22 March 2005.

*We believe that there is a positive relationship between the diversity of secondary pro-*
*vision and higher standards. We want to extend the opportunities available for*
*alternative providers of secondary education to set up schools. It is particularly*
*important to create increased choice at a time when local authorities are taking a*
*strategic view of their provisions and planning reorganisations as part of the 'Build-*
*ing Schools for the Future' programme. The programme offers local authorities an*
*opportunity to reorganise provision in a way that fulfils the long-term vision for edu-*
*cation. We expect all authorities, in developing their plans for 'Building Schools for*
*the Future', to undertake a root-and-branch review of the nature and pattern of provi-*
*sion in their area to ensure that it meets the needs of communities.*

*The programme is designed to drive innovation and transformation in education. To*
*secure their participation in the programme, local authorities, working with other*
*stakeholders, must come forward with bold plans that demonstrate their commitment*

*to those objectives. We therefore expect that local authorities' plans will entail the closure of some existing schools and the establishment of new ones. As I have already explained, local authorities will normally have to hold competitions whenever proposals are required to establish a school.*

*More generally, 'Building Schools for the Future' guidance requires local authorities to consider how to secure a diverse range of schools in their areas. We expect local authorities fully to explore the options for introducing innovative approaches to school management, including an evaluation of academy options. Local authorities will also wish to consider other ways of involving new partners in providing new schools. [Section] 66 allows local authorities to hold competitions voluntarily, even if they were not required to hold one.*

*The Department and our delivery partner for the programme, 'Partnerships for Schools', challenge local authorities to show how their proposed capital investment will translate into demonstrable educational benefits. Authorities are not allowed to proceed with their plans until they have done so.*

*The Government have a joined-up approach to promoting diversity in the provision of schools. The school organisation provisions of the [Act] mean that local authorities will not normally be able to set up schools without inviting a range of providers to make proposals. The programme challenges local authorities to reorganise provision in their areas and provides resources to fund new schools. Together, the measures will guarantee that new providers have many opportunities to establish schools and to increase the choice of schools available to pupils and parents.*

However, concerns were expressed in the parliamentary debate about the additional time it will take to bring about school organisation changes, including the difficulties schools will find themselves in while a competition is happening. For example, staff at an existing community school, which is put forward for rebuilding under BSF, may not know whether the school will be taken over by a promoter or perhaps become a faith school. The then Parliamentary Secretary (Derek Twigg MP) gave the following written answer.

*Competitions for replacement secondary schools will take place only where the local authority decides that statutory proposals for a new secondary school are necessary. The time scale will therefore be the same as for any other reorganisation, with the addition of four months for prospective promoters to prepare their bids. We would expect the local authority to take this into account in planning future reorganisations and discussing them with schools.*

*Since competitions will take place only where proposals for new schools would be required in any case, there should be no increased pressure on staff, parents and pupils. The competition requirement, and increased time for preparation of possible alternative options and provision for people to comment on those proposals, will together give greater opportunities for staff, pupils and parents to have a say about the type of school that they believe will best meet local needs.*

Commons Written Answer, 10 March 2005, col. 1973

# Summary of part 2

The new law on competitions is in ss. 64 to 66 and schedule 10. All proposals for new secondary schools will be subject to a competition to determine which body (local authority, faith group or non-religious charity) should establish the new school. Previously, the Education Act 2002 had only asked that additional secondary schools should be subject to a competition. The 2005 Act also gives the School Organisation Committee (SOC) a duty to decide the result of the competition, although the Secretary of State retains a reserve power to direct that the Office of the Schools Adjudicator determine the outcome. This will happen anyway if the SOC cannot agree. As a consequence of the new law on school competitions, the law on school rationalisation proposals required by the Secretary of State has been re-enacted and now appears in s. 67 and schedule 11. The law on establishing a new school as part of a federation is re-enacted in s. 68. Section 69 prevents LEAs in England from establishing schools in Wales, and LEAs in Wales from establishing schools in England. Sections 70, on closing rural primary schools, and 71, on proposals relating to special schools, were added to the legislation following Government defeats in the House of Lords. Section 72 and schedule 12 make further amendments to school organisation legislation, mainly in response to the new law on competitions for new secondary schools. Section 73 contains statutory definitions.

## Section 64: proposals not requiring the consent of the Secretary of State

Section 28 of SSFA 1998 contains the statutory basis for proposals for new schools: the LEA for community and foundation schools, and the 'promoters' (faith group or non-religious charity) for a new foundation or voluntary school. Section 64 of the 2005 Act amends s. 28 so that it can no longer be used to make proposals for a new secondary school, but with two minor exceptions: 16–19 schools (sixth-form colleges) and 'middle deemed secondary' schools where pupils leave before year 11.

Section 64(2) removes amendments made to s. 28 of the SSFA 1998 by the Education Act 2002 on school competitions and s. 64(3) inserts a new subsection (2A) in s. 28 that stops it being used to propose a new secondary school. Section 64(3) also inserts a new subsection (2B), the effect of which is twofold. There must be a competition for proposed middle schools with pupils in the last year of compulsory schooling but proposals for LEA-maintained sixth-form colleges are excluded from the competition requirements. Middle schools were excluded from the 2002 Act competitions. Consequential changes to the definition of a middle school are made in Schedule 12, paras 1 and 4. Paragraph 4 uses the phrase 'relevant upper age (in relation to a middle school)' in order to define those middle school proposals which must be subject to a competition. Currently, there are six middle schools with year 11 pupils in England. They are in different authorities (Lords Written Parliamentary Answer, 9 February 2005).

## Section 65: publication of proposals with the consent of the Secretary of State

Section 65 adds a new s. 28A (Proposals for the establishment of a community, foundation or voluntary school maintained by an English LEA) to the SSFA 1998.

Under subsection (1) of the new s. 28A, an LEA or a promoter is required to seek the permission of the Secretary of State before publishing proposals to establish a secondary school to be maintained by an English LEA otherwise than under the new competitions proposed in s. 66. In other words, it will continue to be possible to publish proposals for a new secondary school without going through the competition procedure, but it requires the specific permission of the Secretary of State. The new section 28A mirrors section 28 but with changes to take account of the fact that section 28A deals only with the establishment of new secondary schools and not alterations. When consulting on the legislation, the DfES (8 July 2004), indicated that the Secretary of State would give permission under this section for a competition not to be held where:

*...an LEA proposes to establish a school to replace a weak or failing school (especially if this is part of a collaborative restart supported by the Department); where a school with a religious character is proposed to replace a school without such a character; where an independent school comes into the maintained sector; and where promoters propose to establish a new school to increase diversity rather than to meet the general need for places in the area. LEAs will continue to be able to pursue the option of an Academy in their area at any time including to replace an existing school, and where this is their preferred option a competition will not be required.*

## Section 66: proposals for new secondary schools in England

Section 66 gives the LEA the power to publish a notice inviting proposals for the establishment of a secondary school that is a foundation or voluntary school, or an academy. The notice must identify a site for the school, a final date for the receipt of proposals, and any other prescribed information. Proposals must be submitted to the LEA and regulations can prescribe timing, manner of publication and the information to be published. Schedule 10 is added to the Act. Section 66 replaces s. 70 of the 2002 Act.

Section 66(1) makes clear that 'any' new secondary school proposal is captured by the new provision and not just proposals to establish an 'additional' secondary school under s. 70(7) of the 2002 Act.

Section 66(2) provides that the competition notice cannot invite support for an LEA proposal to establish a new community school (as it can under s. 70(2)(a) of the 2002 Act) but the LEA can still (under s. 66(8)(b)) publish its own proposals for a community or foundation school when publishing proposals submitted by other bodies.

Section 66(3) prescribes the information that the competition notice must contain, such as the school site and other matters relating to the school.

Section 66(4) requires the LEA to consult locally before publishing the notice. The Secretary of State can prescribe who must be consulted.

Section 66(7) to (9) states that proposals must contain information to be prescribed by the Secretary of State, that the LEA must publish all proposals received and the timing and manner of the publication (which will be determined by the Secretary of State in regulations).

Under section 66(10), the Secretary of State has power to make regulations requiring LEAs to promote public awareness of received proposals.

Section 66(12) adds schedule 10 to the Act, and s. 66(13) enables an LEA to propose that the new secondary school be situated in the area of another LEA.

## Schedule 10: proposals under section 66 for establishment of secondary schools: supplementary

Schedule 10 is similar to the existing law in schedule 8 of the 2002 Act. However, the decision on the result of the competition will rest with the SOC rather than the Secretary of State. The SOC can, if it so decides, refer all proposals to the adjudicator (para. 4) and must do so if it cannot agree. Under existing legislation there are five (or six) separate groups represented on the SOC, all of which must vote the same way (or abstain) to reach a valid decision (schedule 6 (3) of SSFA 1998). In certain circumstances the Secretary of State can require the proposals to go to the adjudicator (para. 5). The Secretary of State will still have a role with regard to the approval of academies (para. 7) and, as a consequence of the SSFA, will have to approve the religious character of any new faith school. Paragraphs 9 to 15 deal with the implementation of proposals.

### Approval of proposals by SOC or adjudicator

Paragraph 3 states that the Secretary of State can make comments on the submission of proposals to the SOC. The regulations can require the LEA to collect and forward to the SOC any objections or comments.

Paragraph 4 sets out the scope of the SOC's decision-making powers (subject to certain exceptions (see notes on para. 5 below). Subparagraph (2) enables the SOC to reject all the proposals, approve one of the proposals with or without modification, or if the SOC thinks it appropriate, refer all the proposals to the adjudicator. Subparagraphs (4) and (5) deal with linked proposals about school reorganisation and further details will be set out in regulations. This will be particularly beneficial to an LEA removing a middle school tier of provision as decisions on new primary schools can be related to decisions on new secondary schools: linking related decisions is necessary in many school reorganisation proposals, such as moving a secondary school to a new site (which does not require a competition) and amalgamating two secondary schools (which does require a competition).

Subparagraph (6) requires the SOC to have regard to guidance from the Secretary of State on deciding whether or not to approve the result of a competition.

Paragraph 5 gives the Secretary of State a general regulation making power (in subparagraph (1)) or a specific direction power (in subparagraph (2)) to require proposals to be determined by the adjudicator. The RIA states that this power is necessary because some SOCs have of a poor record of decision-making: 'There is a risk of controversy in areas where the SOC's judgement or impartiality is not respected.' The RIA goes on to record that:

> A SOC would be regarded as having a record of poor decision making when one or more of the following criteria had been met: (i) failure to comply with regulations gov-

*erning SOC procedures; (ii) failure to ensure that those bringing forward proposals had complied with regulations governing the publication of proposals; (iii) disregarding the Secretary of State's guidance on decision-making, particularly the sections related to the importance of extending choice through encouraging the expansion of popular and successful schools and the establishment of new schools that add to the diversity and quality of provision or (iv) taking unreasonable decisions (i.e. decisions that no reasonable person would have taken in the light of the evidence available).*
(page 56)

The SOC is required to refer any linked proposals (see para. 4) to the adjudicator and complete consultation with the Secretary of State if there is a proposal for an academy (see para. 7). Paragraph 6 requires the adjudicator to consider afresh proposals arising from the competition.

Paragraph 7 deals with any proposal involving an academy. The SOC cannot approve a proposal involving an academy unless the Secretary of State has indicated a willingness to enter into an agreement with promoters to establish it. The same applies to an adjudicator. Approval of an Academy by the SOC does not oblige the Secretary of State to enter into an agreement to establish an academy.

### LEA determination of community school proposal

In part 3, para. 9 maintains the longstanding position that an LEA school organisation proposals that receive no objections, or if there are objections, they are withdrawn after discussion, can be implemented. If the only proposal following a competition is a community school or a foundation school to be established by the LEA, then the matter does not have to be considered further by the SOC and the LEA can determine to implement the proposed secondary school.

### Implementation of proposals

In part 4, para. 10 requires approved proposals to be implemented. The provision is very similar to para. 5 of schedule 8 of the 2002 Act with the SOC replacing the Secretary of State role. Paragraph 11 provides for the case where the SOC determines (under para. 10(3)) that implementing the proposals would be unreasonably difficult or the circumstances have altered such that implementing the proposals would be inappropriate. Paragraphs 12–15 deal with the different circumstances of implementing a proposal relating to a community school, a foundation or voluntary-controlled school, a voluntary-aided school or an academy, respectively.

## Section 67 and schedule 11: rationalisation of school places in England

Local education authorities have been able to propose to rationalise school place provision since their establishment. However, in the early 1990s, the Government believed that local authorities were not doing enough to remove empty school places. It was also recognised that it would be difficult to do so if there were a significant number of grant-maintained schools. Sections 232 to 237 of the Education Act 1993 first gave the Secretary of State power to require LEAs to come up with plans either to remove or increase school places. If LEAs, or governors of voluntary and foundation schools, do not submit proposals, or the Secretary of State does not believe the locally produced proposals will work, he/she can make his/her own proposals. The law specifies how the Secretary of State's proposals will be handled, including provision for the adjudicator to hold a local inquiry into the proposals.

The law was consolidated into sections 500 to 505 of the Education Act 1996 and recast as schedule 7 of the SSFA 1998. The Government has taken the opportunity of the 2005 Act to rewrite the law again to take account of competitions for secondary schools. Section 71 of the Education Act 2002 made a poor attempt at taking account of academies in school rationalisation proposals in England (academies cannot be created in Wales) and is repealed by the 2005 Act. Schedule 11 (of the 2005 Act) consolidates the position in England while amendments in schedule 12 (of the 2005 Act) make consequential amendments to schedule 7 of the SSFA 1998 so that it now only applies in Wales. LEA rationalisation plans can only propose an academy, not close one, in response to a direction from the Secretary of State to remove school places.

The law has not been tested, as reported by the then Parliamentary Secretary at the DfES (Derek Twigg MP) in debate on the Bill. He went on to justify keeping these powers as they 'have proved useful for demonstrating our [the Government's] commitment to the proper supply of certain school places and for requiring action if it is not taken voluntarily' (Commons Hansard, Standing Committee A, col. 72, 22 March 2005).

Given that the legislation has never been used and, judging by the Minister's comments, the threat of using the legislation is sufficient to make LEAs and voluntary and foundation schools come into line, further comment is not merited.

## Section 68: proposals for establishment of federated school

Section 68 enables a new school or schools to become part of a federation on establishment and replaces s. 74 of the Education Act 2002. Section 74(2), which is a power to modify, by regulation, other primary legislation to enable a new school to be established as a federated school, is not re-enacted because of other powers in the 2005 Act. (See comments on s.124, page 70.)

## Section 69: LEA not to establish a school on the opposite side of the Welsh border

An LEA in England cannot establish a school in Wales and an LEA in Wales cannot establish a school in England. No England LEA maintains a school in Wales (Lords Written Answer, col. WA117, 9 February 2005).

## Section 70: closing rural primary schools

Section 70 was added following a Government defeat in the House of Lords, although the final wording is the result of a Government amendment in the Commons. A new subsection (4A) replaces the existing subsection (4) in s. 29 of the SSFA 1998. In formulating a proposal to close a rural primary school the LEA for any school, or the governing body for a voluntary or foundation school, must consider the effect of closure on the local community, implications for transport including the increased use of motor vehicles and pupils' travel to other schools consequent on closure, and any alternatives to closure. Before a closure notice is published consultation must take place with parents, the district council in shire areas and any parish council. The Secretary of State receives an order making power to designate primary schools as 'rural'.

In debate on the Bill, the then Parliamentary Secretary at the Wales Office (Don Touhig MP) stated: 'Although the protection that it offers is not, in our view, really necessary, since most of it was copied from existing guidance, we are not opposed to its provisions for that same reason' (Commons Hansard, Standing Committee A, col. 73 to 74, 22 March 2005).

## Section 71: Making changes to special schools

Section 71 was added following a Government defeat in the House of Lords, although the final wording is the result of a Government amendment in the Commons. A new subsection (4A) replaces the existing subsection (4) in s. 31 of the SSFA 1998. In formulating a proposal to make a 'prescribed alteration', the LEA for any maintained special school, and the governing body for a foundation special school, must consult parents and any LEA that has placed children at the school.

## Section 72 and schedule 12: school organisation: further amendments

Section 72 adds schedule 12 to the Act containing further amendments. Some have already been referred to, for example paras 1 and 4 and the new definition of a middle school (see comments on s. 64 earlier). Most are updates of statutory references to do with secondary school competitions or school rationalisation.

Paragraph 2 is consequential on the new secondary school competition rules. If a local authority accepts a school property on trust (and the local authority acts as trustees) under s. 529 of the Education Act 1996, then the school must be a community school. However, the LEA must publish a notice to establish the school as a community school, which may now be done under the new s. 28A of the SSFA 1998 and the new section 66 of the Education Act 2005.

Paragraphs 13(4) and 13(6) are new. Paragraph 13(4) inserts a new subparagraph (6D) into para. 3 of schedule 6 to the SSFA 1998. It enables regulations to be made that limit the time which a SOC can consider a proposal before referral to the adjudicator. This presumably is to require a SOC to take a decision on, for example, a contentious local issue within a specific time. Similarly, para. 13(6) inserts a new subparagraph (6B) into para. 5 of schedule 6 to the 1998 Act. The Secretary of State can make regulations to put a time limit on a SOC's consideration of a modification to an approved proposal.

## Section 73: interpretation of part 2

This section contains statutory definitions.

# Part 3  Training the school workforce

## Introduction

The Act renames the Teacher Training Agency (TTA) as the Training and Development Agency for Schools (TDA) and extends its work to cover the whole school workforce as part of the Government's school workforce reforms.

The Education Act 1994 established the TTA to be a funding agency for initial teacher training in England, removing this responsibility from the Higher Education Funding Council for England (HEFCE). In addition, the TTA was required to contribute to raising teaching standards, promote teaching as a career, improve the quality and efficiency of initial teacher training (ITT) and other routes into teaching, secure the involvement of schools in initial teacher training, and generally secure that teachers are well fitted and trained for their task. The TTA also promotes the continuing professional development (CPD) of teachers.

The Education Act 2002 effectively extended the remit of the TTA by making it clear that a range of adults working in schools, such as teaching assistants and learning support assistants, are 'teachers' (although not qualified teachers). This change provided the legal basis for the TTA's work with higher level teaching assistants (HLTAs). The then Secretary of State for Education and Skills (Charles Clarke) announced on 29 March 2004 the new role for the TTA, which was to maximise the skills of the whole teaching workforce and play a key part in a wider network to train and support all staff working with children, as outlined in the Every Child Matters reforms. See DfES News: *Clarke congratulates Teacher Training Agency and announces enhanced role* (Clarke, 2004).

Of the 27 sections in part 3, nine apply solely to Wales and are not described here. The majority of these sections clarify the role of the TTA in Wales, especially its relationship with the National Assembly for Wales and the Higher Education Funding Council for Wales (HEFCW).

The 2005 Act repeals all the provisions on teacher training in the 1994 Act with the exception of s. 11A (which prescribes the general duty of the Secretary of State to secure that sufficient facilities are available for training teachers) and s. 18 (an historic provision to safeguard payments made to lecturers in closed teacher training colleges). Section

18A (on the inspection of teaching training) is replaced by new inspection provisions: found in ss. 18B (for England) and 18C (for Wales) by schedule 14 of the 2005 Act (see comments on s. 98 on page 50).

# The Training and Development Agency for Schools

Sections 74 to 77 and schedule 13 set up and specify the functions and membership of the TDA. Sections 78 to 80 contain the funding rules of the TDA. Sections 81 and 82 contain the powers of the Secretary of State and Welsh Assembly to fund the TDA and HEFCW, respectively. Section 83 gives the TDA a general power to do anything to further its objectives and s. 84 enables the Secretary of State and the Welsh Assembly to give directions to the TDA.

## Section 74: the Training and Development Agency for Schools

The Teacher Training Agency is renamed the Training and Development Agency for Schools to reflect the new role in relation to training and development for the whole school workforce.

## Section 75: functions of the Agency

The TTA's objectives were previously set out in section 1(2) of the 1994 Act. These are repeated in section 75(2) but enlarged, with the exception of (d), to cover the whole school workforce, namely to:

a) contribute to raising the standards of teaching and of other activities carried out by the school workforce

b) promote careers in the school workforce

c) improve the quality and efficiency of all routes into the school workforce

d) secure the involvement of schools in all courses and programmes for the initial training of school teachers.

Section 75(3) provides the context for the Agency's functions, namely to secure that the school workforce is well fitted and trained to:

a) promote the spiritual, moral, behavioural, social, cultural, mental and physical development of children and young people

b) contribute to their well-being

c) prepare them for the opportunities, responsibilities and experiences of later life.

Section 75(4) links the definition of 'well-being' to that in section 10(2) of the Children Act 2004 and the 'five outcomes' (see section 2 on page 11, for a list of the five outcomes).

Section 75(5) defines the school workforce, namely persons who work in schools and persons who do not work in schools but whose work involves teaching. The latter will mean that a range of teachers working in school support services, such as teachers who provide home teaching services, and those who work in outdoor centres, libraries and museums, will be covered.

## Section 76: powers of the Agency in Wales

The rules and procedures for the Agency's work in Wales are found in s. 76.

## Section 77: membership, etc. of the Agency

The size limits on the membership of the Agency have been removed as have the rules about requiring experience of teaching in schools, teaching in higher education etc. The Secretary of State continues to appoint the members of the Agency.

## Schedule 13: the Training and Development Agency for Schools

Schedule 13 sets out the duties and powers of the Agency, how its proceedings should be conducted and the conditions of appointment, tenure and the remuneration of members of the Agency. There are no significant changes from schedule 1 to the 1994 Act which it replaces.

## Section 78: powers of the Agency to provide financial support

The TTA currently has powers to provide financial support under s. 5 of the 1994 Act, orders made under section 16 of that Act and regulations made under section 50 of the Education (No. 2) Act 1986. These powers are replaced by ss. 78 to 80 of the 2005 Act. Section 78(1) enables the Agency to provide any person with financial support, as the Agency thinks fit, providing that the financial support is in keeping with the objectives described in s. 75(2) (see page 45). Section 78(2) makes clear that financial support can be provided to individual members of the school workforce, persons training to be members of the school workforce, providers of training for the school workforce (for example, initial teacher training institutions and school-centred ITT providers) and employers of members of the school workforce.

## Section 79: forms of financial support under section 78

Section 79 enables the Agency to attach terms and conditions to financial support. Sections 79(4) and (5) allow the Agency to control fees charged by training providers, although an updating of the statutory reference in schedule 14(25) makes clear that that the Agency's power in this respect is constrained by the Secretary of State's duty to control fees under section 23 of the Higher Education Act 2004. In s. 79(7) the Agency must take account of any other forecast of demand for members of the school workforce supplied by the Secretary of State and on any assessment of the quality of training provided by Ofsted. Previously, this applied only to teachers.

## Section 80: provisions supplementary to sections 78 and 79

Section 80(1) requires the Agency not to fund institutions in such a way as to discourage them from obtaining funding from other sources, such as research and development activity. Section 80(2) requires the Agency to maintain a balance of funding between institutions with a religious character and those without such a character. Section 80(3) enables the Agency to obtain information from training providers.

## Section 81: grants to the Agency by the Secretary of State

Section 81 largely re-enacts the Secretary of State's power to fund the Agency under s. 7 of the 1994 Act. Section 80(4) prevents the Secretary of State from imposing terms and conditions relating to the admission of students or the selection of staff as a condition of funding although this will now apply to any course for members, or potential members, of the school workforce.

## Section 82: grants to the Agency by the Welsh Assembly

This is a Wales-only provision.

## Section 83: non-funding functions of the Agency

The Agency acquires a new power under s. 83(1) to do anything it thinks fit in furtherance of its objectives. Previously, the Secretary of State had to make an order specifying the additional functions, for example giving the TTA the power to provide training for adults on the

Graduate Teacher Training Programme. Twelve orders have been made in the last ten years and this change will improve flexibility. The TDA will be able to borrow money, although this will require the permission of the Secretary of State under schedule 13(1). Section 83(2) allows the TDA to provide information, advice and other services outside England and Wales and s. 83(3) allows it to charge for information, advice and other services.

### Section 84: directions by the Secretary of State and Welsh Assembly

The TDA will be subject both to general and specific directions made by the Secretary of State (and the Assembly in Wales). This power replaces s. 8 of the 1994 Act, which has not been used but could, for example, be used to give general directions about financial management in higher education institutions providing ITT, or could relate specifically to financial mismanagement in a named institution. The direction has to be made by order that requires a statutory instrument under section 120 giving a relatively high level of parliamentary scrutiny.

# Funding of teacher training by the Higher Education Funding Council for Wales

Sections 85 to 91 deal with the funding of teacher training in Wales.

# Common provisions

### Section 92: joint exercise of functions

Section 92(1) replaces s. 9 of the 1994 Act. It enables the TDA and, in Wales the HEFCW (collectively called the funding agencies in this section), to work jointly with HEFCE and the LSC (and its Welsh equivalent). Under s. 92(3), the Secretary of State can permit the Agency to work jointly with other bodies. LEAs' general powers allow them to work with the TDA on, for example, promoting teaching as a career, and therefore they are not named here.

### Section 93: efficiency studies

The TDA can do research, and work with others on research, aimed at improving the economy, efficiency and effectiveness of training providers. The training providers must cooperate with the researchers. This replaces s.10 of the 1994 Act.

## Section 94: duty to provide information

The TDA is under a duty to provide information to the Secretary of State as requested and may provide other information as the TDA thinks fit. Persons (which will include training providers and LEAs) who have received, or applied for, grants, etc. from the TDA must supply information as requested. This replaces s.15 of the 1994 Act.

# Provision of training in schools

## Section 95: power of maintained schools to provide training for the school workforce

Governing bodies of maintained schools can provide training for members of the school workforce (s. 95(1)). This is an extension of the power under which schools could provide training for teachers under s.12 of the 1994 Act. Training can be provided for the school staff alone or in partnership with other schools and training providers. Section 95 provides the statutory basis of school-centred ITT and will no doubt in future enable schools to provide this for other members of the school workforce. The power is needed by schools to provide courses specifically funded by the TDA, especially where trainees are not their own employees at the time of the training.

The training provided by governing bodies may or may not be higher education (s. 95(2)). Expenditure is not to be treated as 'expenditure for the purpose of the school' and is outside the delegated school funding mechanism (s. 95(4)). The rules on schools providing further education do not apply (s. 95(5)) and s. 95 does not affect the normal business of schools in providing professional development for all staff (s. 95(6)).

# Supplementary

## Section 96: interpretation of references to training

This section defines 'training' in this Act and includes training or education to enable a person to be a member of the school workforce, a better teacher or other member of the school workforce, and any connected assessment relating to the award of a qualification. Section 96 defines 'training' in other education legislation as relating to teachers, or potential teachers, only.

## Section 97: institutions of a denominational character

Defines which institutions have a religious character for the purpose of section 80. Higher education institutions must have a quarter of their governing body appointed to represent a religion or religious denomination to meet the criterion. For schools, it is one fifth and therefore will capture voluntary-controlled schools. Other definitions are provided, which relate to the ownership of property.

## Section 98 and schedule 14: further amendments relating to the training of the school workforce

Consequential amendments are made in schedule 14 to other legislation to reflect the change of name of the TTA to the TDA, and the change of function to cover the school workforce and fund training providers.

Schedule 14(13) deals with the inspection of teacher training and adds a new section 18B to the 1994 Act and repeals the existing section 18A. Ofsted can inspect initial and in-service training for teachers, and specialist teaching assistants, provided by training providers. The term 'specialist teaching assistant' is not defined. It is noteworthy that Ofsted does not receive the power to inspect training provision for the whole school workforce, only for teachers and specialist teaching assistants. Statutory references are updated to cover the new TDA and the new role of Ofsted in school inspection in part 1 of the 2005 Act. This means that Ofsted could not inspect a higher education training course for, for example, school bursars, although training provided in schools might be covered by the law on school inspection.

Schedule 14(23) updates the definition of training (in s. 14 of the 2002 Act) for the powers of the Secretary of State to give financial assistance, to match the definition used in part 3 of this Act. In other words, the Secretary of State has equivalent powers to the TDA to fund the initial and in-service training of members of the school workforce.

## Section 99 and schedule 15: transitional provisions

This section contains supporting legislation to allow for a smooth transfer from the TTA to the TDA.

## Section 100: interpretation of part 3 of the 2005 Act

This section contains statutory definitions.

# Part 4  Miscellaneous

## Maintained schools

The Act brings together several changes concerning the management of schools maintained by LEAs. Section 101 and schedule 16 introduce the new ring-fenced DSG from April 2006. Section 102 enables targets to be set on the performance of LEAs. Sections 103 and 104 abolish the current requirements for reports and annual parents' meetings and substitute a requirement for the new *School Profile*. Section 105 allows schools to provide higher education. Section 106 makes special provision to give looked-after children priority in school admissions. Section 107 places restrictions on the disposal of land by foundation schools.

### Section 101 and schedule 16: funding of maintained schools

There is insufficient space here to do more than give a brief indication of recent changes to the law on school funding in order to set the 2005 Act changes in context. However, fuller expositions of the overall history and previous legislation are available elsewhere. See, for example, *What is the LEA for?* (Whitbourn *et al.*, 2004, pp. 165 to 190) and *A Guide to the Education Act 2002* (Fowler with Evans, 2002, pp. 12 and 13).

The principal legislation on school funding is the SSFA 1998. Following a two-year review of local government finance including a specific review of school funding, the Education Act 2002 made significant changes to the 1998 Act. The principal change, found in s. 45B of the 1998 Act, was to empower the Secretary of State to set a minimum schools budget for each LEA. The 'schools budget' was defined in a new s. 45A as, roughly, all expenditure on pupils whether at school or otherwise but excluding expenditure that the LEA needed for its business called the 'LEA budget'. The 'individual schools budget' is the sum left after the LEA has deducted from the 'schools budget' items of central expenditure on pupils. Schools receive a 'budget share' of the 'individual schools budget', which is an annual sum determined according to rules derived from s. 47 of the 1998 Act. The 2002 Act also required a Schools Forum to be established to have an advisory role in relation to authorities' school funding arrangements. This provision is found in s. 47A of the 1998 Act.

The school funding 'crisis' in the early summer of 2003 changed everything. In spite of what was claimed to be a record increase in national resources devoted to education for the 2003/04 financial year, the headteacher associations reported that the money was not getting through to schools. There followed an acrimonious debate between headteachers, local authorities and DfES ministers about what had happened, with the debate focusing on whether local authorities had 'passported' the national increase in resources to schools. The Government changed the rules for the 2004/05 financial year and also changed the law, by way of the Local Government Act 2003, to require local authorities to submit their budgets to the Secretary of State earlier to allow for greater vetting. The result was the minimum funding guarantee, a requirement to deliver a minimum percentage increase in every school's 'budget share', and a limit on the increase in expenditure on items of central expenditure not delegated to schools within the 'schools budget'. Local authorities can apply to the Secretary of State for relief from these provisions, and many have done so.

The Government's *Five Year Strategy for Children and Learners* (DfES, 2004a) announced new funding arrangements for schools from the 2006/07 financial year. The principal elements are:

- the removal of school funding from local authority finance, although local authorities will still be responsible for delivering the money to schools through a ring-fenced DSG

- three-year budgets, based on the academic year, for all maintained schools, geared to pupil numbers, with a guaranteed minimum increase each year.

The White Paper offered schools 'unprecedented practical financial security and freedom to schools in their forward planning'. The Government aimed 'to ensure there are no adverse effects for the rest of local government' through the removal of the Revenue Support Grant currently paid to local authorities on the basis of Schools Formula Spending Share (SFSS) allocations.

Section 95 introduces schedule 16, which contains the main changes to the legislation. Further provisions relating to changing the basis of budgeting from the financial year to the academic year are contained in schedule 18. The DfES provided comprehensive information on the changes when the Bill was published (www.teachernet.gov.uk/docbank/index.cfm?id=7945). The DfES consultation on implementation (www.teachernet.gov.uk/management/schoolfunding/2006-07_funding_arrangements/) also includes key sections of the 1998 Act, showing the effect of the 2005 Act changes. The principal changes affecting England are on three-year budgets, payment of grant to LEAs and decision-making powers for the Schools Forum.

NB: Wales uses the same legislative basis for school funding as England, that is ss. 45 to 53 of the 1998 Act. Much of the new legislation separates the school funding arrangements for England and Wales, although the 2005 Act does allow the Welsh Assembly to adopt the new England arrangements without recourse to further primary legislation.

### Three-year budgets

Amendments to enable three-year budgeting can be found in schedule 16, paras 2 to 6 (which amend ss. 45, 45A and 47 the 1998 Act) and schedule 18, paras 5 to 12 and 14 (which amend s. 494 of the 1996 Act (on recoupment), ss. 48, 50, 51A, 52 and schedule 15 of the 1998 Act (on school and LEA funding), s. 7 of the Learning and Skills Act 2000 (on funding school sixth forms), and s. 37 of the 2002 Act (on payments in respect of dismissals, etc.)).

With one exception, the term 'financial year' is replaced by 'funding period' although the default funding period is the financial year. The exception is schedule 18, para. 10 (financial statements), which enables the Secretary of State to require LEAs to prepare budget and outturn statements. The term 'financial year' is replaced by 'prescribed period', enabling the Secretary of State to adjust the requirements in relation both to budget and outturn statements as necessary to reflect the determination of budgets on a three-year, academic year basis. It also allows flexibility for school budgets to be allocated and accounted for either on an academic year or on the normal financial year.

Schedule 16, para. 4 inserts a new s. 45AA (power to require LEAs in England to determine schools budget) into the 1998 Act. Regulations under this new section can:

- require each LEA to set the 'schools budget' for a funding period up to 48 months before the beginning of the funding period

- make provision for the budget thus set to be redetermined before the funding period begins

- impose requirements for notifying governing bodies of the authority's schools budget.

The purpose of this provision, according to the *Explanatory Notes*, is to require LEAs 'to set schools' budgets at specified dates for a number of periods which total three years, although there would be scope to make later adjustments for each funding period within the total'.

Schedule 16, para. 6(3) (a) and (4) amend s. 47 of the 1998 Act (determination of budget shares). This enables individual schools' budget shares to be calculated for funding periods that start up to 48 months after a prescribed date, with provision for such budget shares for each period to be redetermined before the start of the funding period in question, if necessary. According to the *Explanatory Notes*, regulations could enable budget shares to be redetermined during the funding period to reflect, for example, data changes. However, the effect of data changes could be carried over to a subsequent funding period in the form of retrospective adjustments. Paragraph 6(3)(c) requires governing bodies to be notified of schools' budget shares and any redetermination.

It is worth pointing out that despite the references to 'three-year budgets' the interaction of this with the two-year cycle of government spending reviews will mean a three-year planning horizon only every other year. In alternate years schools will have a budget that lasts 2 years and 5 months.

### Payment of grant

Schedule 16, paragraph 3(5), puts beyond doubt that the Secretary of State can grant aid an LEA under s. 14 (Power of Secretary of State to give financial assistance) of the 2002 Act and expect the whole of the grant to be applied to the 'schools budget'. Although the term is not given statutory recognition, this grant is referred to as the 'dedicated schools grant' (DSG). The term 'dedicated schools budget' has also been used although in future the 'schools budget' will contain the 'dedicated schools grant' plus any additional funding the local authority wishes to contribute from its other resources.

The Government met concerns about Parliamentary scrutiny of the new arrangements through schedule 16, paragraph 8, which makes the first set of regulations for the new arrangements subject to an affirmative resolution of both Houses of Parliament.

Schedule 16, paragraphs 3(8) and 5, repeal the LEA duty to notify the Secretary of State of the proposed 'schools budget' and the Secretary of State's power to determine a minimum schools budget. The new sections 45B and 45C apply only to Wales.

### Schools Forum

The extent to which an LEA may deduct expenditure from the schools budget (that is, retain funding to spend on pupil-related provision which is managed centrally rather than delegating it to individual schools in the form of budget shares) is subject to control through regulations which may set limits on the size of specified types of expenditure or set other conditions. Any variation on this has so far had to be allowed by amending regulations which has happened frequently. The 2005 Act enables such decisions, within limits, to be approved by the schools forum with an appeal to the Secretary of State.

Schedule 16, paragraph 7, amends the description of schools forums' functions in section 47A of the 1998 Act so as to include the exercise of the new powers to approve certain LEA proposals conferred on schools forums, by paragraphs 3(7) and 6(3)(d) of schedule 16.

Schedule 16, paragraph 3(7), allows regulations to make provision for an LEA to apply to their schools forum or the Secretary of State for approval to make deductions not otherwise authorised in the regulations. This may relate either to a higher deduction for specific items, or the total of deducted items, or the deduction of items not normally permitted by the regulations. The *Explanatory Notes* states that for England it is intended that regulations will only allow an LEA to deduct an amount less than a national limit. If the forum does not authorise the LEA's proposals, the authority will have the right to make an application to the Secretary of State. A schools forum will not be able to originate and approve its own proposals for central spend; it may only approve those put forward by its LEA. For the City of London and the Isles of Scilly (which do not have schools forums) such applications would be made direct to the Secretary of State.

At present the Secretary of State may authorise (but not require) arrangements for calculating schools' budget shares which vary from those normally permitted by the regulations made under section 47 of the 1998 Act. Schedule 16, paragraph 6(3)(d), provides that regulations may extend this power to schools forums. Again, the proposal must be made by the LEA, and regulations will provide that if the forum does not approve the proposal, the local education authority may apply instead to the Secretary of State. The *Explanatory Notes* state that regulations will allow schools forums to approve only limited variations in the operation of the minimum funding guarantee in respect of individual schools or groups of schools to avoid them receiving anomalous budget shares.

## Section 102: LEA targets for England

The Children Act 2004 consolidated a number of statutory plans into a Children and Young People's Plan (section 17) and repealed, from 1st March 2005, the duty on LEAs to produce the following plans: children's services, behaviour support, class size reduction, education development, school organisation, early years development and childcare, and adoption services (schedule 5, part 1). A consequence of this was the removal of the Secretary of State's power to agree targets with LEAs contained in the education development plan legislation. The Secretary of State has decided that this power is necessary and it is re-provided in section 102. The Secretary of State has the power (s.102(1)) to make regulations to require LEAs to set annual targets on the educational performance of pupils at maintained schools and also of children looked-after by the local authority whether those children attend schools maintained by the LEA or not. Section 102(2) sets out the issues to be covered in regulations, including the matters to which the targets must relate and the timetable for setting and submitting the targets to the Secretary of State.

The DfES had not consulted publicly on the regulations. However, the *Regulatory Impact Assessment* states that the targets will cover

- pupil performance in tests at Key Stage 2 and 3;
- pupil performance at GCSE exams and other approved vocational qualifications
- performance by pupils with special educational needs;
- performance by looked after pupils; and,
- attendance at school.

DfES *Children and Young People's Plan: Consultation on Regulations and Guidance* (DfES, 2005a) asks local authorities to continue their normal practice of submitting the statutory education targets to the DfES by the end of January each year. Local authorities should therefore plan to submit targets in January 2006 for the 2007 school year.

## Section 103: removal of requirements for governors' reports and parents' meetings

Section 103(1) removes the requirement on school governing bodies in England to produce an annual report under section 30 of the Education Act 2002. Schools will, though, have to produce a *School Profile* under section104 (see below). In recent years the contents of the annual report and the school prospectus (a publication for parents of prospective pupils) have become similar. Schools are still (as at June 2005) under a duty to produce a prospectus (under the Education (School Information) (England) Regulations 2002, SI 2002/2897 made under section 537 (Power of Secretary of State to require information from governing bodies etc.)); although the *Regulatory Impact Assessment* states that the contents of the prospectus will be deregulated and the DfES consultation on the *School Profile* (26 March 2004) asked whether the *School Profile* could form the basis of the prospectus and what elements of the prospectus might be replaced and repealed.

Section 102(2) repeals the requirement to hold an annual parents' meeting in England. In responding to the charge that the Government was not committed to parental involvement, the then DfES Parliamentary Undersecretary, Lord Filkin, replied that 'it is better for the Government not to prescribe for schools the precise mechanisms through which they should involve parents'. The Government was thinking about what should be done but a 'formulaic process of issuing a dull annual report and having a non-attended annual meeting' was not sufficient (Lords Hansard, 24 Feb 2005: Column 1432).

A consequential amendment on the reporting by governing bodies on implementing their policy for pupils with special educational needs is made in paragarpoh 2 of schedule 18. Section 317 (Duties of governing body or LEA in relation to pupils with special educational needs) of 1996 Act requires governing bodies to include in their annual report information about their SEN policies, and admission of disabled pupils, steps taken to ensure disabled pupils are not treated less favourably etc. These duties are now found in a new s.317(5), (6) and (6A) but without reference to the Governors' Annual Report. The Secretary of State can prescribe the SEN information required to be in the new report.

## Section 104: School Profiles

As part of the vision for a new relationship with schools the then Minister for School Standards (David Miliband) announced (January 2004) the development of a *School Profile* for each school to be produced by the DfES. The aim of the *School Profile* is to supplement data contained in Attainment and Assessment Tables, replace the Governors' Annual Report (see section 103 above) and increase flexibility around elements of the School Prospectus.

DfES consultation *School Profile* (DfES, 2004b) envisaged that the Profile should be in a standardised format for all schools. The Profile

*should be relatively short – perhaps between 2 to 4 sides of A4 – and it should allow for easy comparisons between schools. However, there would be nothing to prevent schools from publishing more information than the Profile contains ... [the Profile would be] compiled and accessed as an electronic document, which could be printed. Much of the basic statistical data could be provided automatically and derived from information already supplied by schools to the DfES or supplied by OFSTED.*

*This would be combined with information provided direct by the Head Teacher and Governing Body of the school. DfES consultation on* School Profile*, paragraphs 3.4 and 3.5*

The consultation document said that the DfES wanted parents, governors and teachers to have access to the Profile via links with government websites although in debate the then Parliamentary Undersecretary, Lord Filkin, stated that statutory guidance will provide for all schools to give a hard copy of the Profile to parents, except where parents have requested information electronically (Lords Hansard, 24 Feb 2005, col 1433).

Section 104 adds a new section 30A (*School Profiles*) to the Education Act 2002. The new section:

- requires governing bodies of maintained schools in England to prepare and publish a *School Profile*

- gives the Secretary of State a power to make regulations prescribing the content, format and manner of publication of the profile, including the frequency with which it is revised and published

- requires governing bodies to have regard to any guidance issued by the Secretary of State in preparing the *School Profile*.

The DfES submission to the House of Lords Committee on Delegated Powers and Regulatory Reform acknowledges that the Government does not intend to use the regulation making powers in this section but will initially rely on issuing statutory guidance. Regulations will only be made if there is 'insufficient self-regulation or inadequacies in the quality of the information provided in the *School Profile*'.

The 2004 consultation indicated that the DfES intended to introduce the *School Profile* from September 2005.

## Section 105: provision and funding of higher education in maintained schools

Schools are prevented from offering any form of higher education, for example a degree level course, by section 1(4) of the Education Act 1996. According to the *Regulatory Impact Assessment*, schools are already providing higher education courses in keeping with the Government's commitment to a learning culture geared to personalised learning. In 2002/03, there were 240 young people in school on the Open University's Young

Applicants in School Scheme. This had risen to 680 young people in 2003/04 in over 60 schools. The Government expects that over time, more schools will offer their pupils some experience of higher education.

In order to clarify the legal position, section 105 allows certain forms of higher education to be provided at schools by inserting a new section 28A into the Education Act 2002. Under the new section, schools will be able to offer higher education courses that fall within paragraph 1(g) or (h) of Schedule 6 to the Education Reform Act 1988. That is schools will be able to provide courses in preparation for a professional examination at higher level or courses providing education at a higher level (whether or not in preparation for an examination)). The *Explanatory Notes* state that the former include vocational or professional courses at level 4 (higher education level) and the latter include modules of first degree courses or components of Higher National Diplomas (HNDs) but not courses resulting in the award of a full first degree or the full HND. A course does not have to be provided by a teacher at the school. Section 28A(2) requires that studying a higher education course must not interfere, to any significant extent, with the pupil's other school education.

## Section 106: admission arrangements to make special provision for looked-after children

The *School Admissions: Code of Practice* (DfES, 2003) recommended that all admission authorities give children in local authority care top priority in their oversubscription criteria (para. 3.14). However, the House of Commons Education and Skills Committee in its 2004 report *Secondary Education: School Admissions* (HC 58-1) (GB. Parliament. HoC, Education and Skills Committee, 2004) reported that admission authorities are setting aside the guidance in the Code of Practice and recommended that the Government seek a regulation making power to compel admission authorities to prioritise children in care. This has been done in s. 106, which inserts a new subsection (1A) after s. 89(1) of the SSFA1998. The Secretary of State will be able to make regulations that require all admission authorities (be they the LEA for community and voluntary-controlled schools or the governing body for voluntary-aided or foundation schools) to ensure that looked-after children are offered admission in preference to other children. It is possible that schools with a religious character may be permitted to restrict priority to looked-after children of the relevant faith.

The Code of Practice is currently being revised and it is expected that a consultation draft will be published later in 2005.

## Section 107 and schedule 17: restrictions on disposal of land

Section 107 and schedule 17 amend schedule 22 to the SSFA1998 to close a loophole on the disposal of publicly funded foundation school land, that is land which was originally provided by a local authority or purchased with the proceeds of disposal of such land. The principle achieved by the legislation is that the Secretary of State must first give permission before a foundation school disposes of any land in all cases. Many foundation schools do not have foundations in which case the land is owned by the governing body not a separate foundation body (as established under s. 21 of the 1998 Act) or trustees. However, if a foundation school subsequently decides to transfer its land to a foundation body or trustees then the foundation body or trustees could dispose of the land without permission of the Secretary of State. The 2005 Act closes this loophole.

This provision is important because of the encouragement given by the DfES in the *Five Year Strategy for Children and Learners* (DfES, 2004a) for community and voluntary-controlled schools to change category and become a foundation school, and for foundation schools without foundations to acquire them, which would mean transferring the land from the school governing body to the foundation's trustees. The s. 105 amendments close a loophole on the transfer of land to trustees after the foundation school has been established. The 1998 Act already covered the case of a foundation school transferring land to trustees on establishment.

# Sharing information

The Government has used the 2005 Act to enable greater sharing of information in three areas: ss. 108 and 109 on education maintenance allowances, ss. 110 to 112 on FSM, and ss. 113 and 114 on school workforce information. The driver is the significantly increased power of information technology in recent years, combined with the Government's wish to reduce bureaucracy, increase efficiency and improve decision making. The business case for each change is described below. Few concerns were raised about the increase in data sharing, with the exception of those raised by the Lords and Commons Joint Committee on Human Rights. The Committee questioned the compatibility of Article 8 of the European Convention on Human Rights (the right to respect for private life) with the creation of a database containing information about the school workforce and to the sharing and disclosure of information contained in the database (Twelfth report, 9 Mar 2005). The Government response is still awaited (at June 2005).

## Section 108: supply of information: education maintenance allowances

Education maintenance allowances (EMAs) were piloted by 56 local authorities from September 1999, and sections 181 to 185 of the Education Act 2002 established a specific statutory basis for the allowances. The Government has subsequently chosen to manage the allowances through a single national private sector organisation, known as the Assessment and Payment Body. The national EMA scheme began in September 2004. The scheme aims to broaden participation, promote the retention of the 16-19 age group in post-compulsory education and to improve their attainment.

Young people aged 16-19 from low-income households who stay in education receive a means-tested EMA. In 2005, the allowance was worth up to £30 per week (plus discretionary bonuses of £100 for completing a course, for example). The means testing is done on household income and involves verifying information held either by the Inland Revenue or the Department for Work and Pensions (DWP).

The purpose of information sharing is to enable the Assessment and Payment Body to determine an applicant's eligibility by verifying income-related information that has been supplied in support of the application. Currently, the applicant has to present a Tax Credit Award Notice or seek written confirmation from the DWP on his/her family's social security benefits. The *Regulatory Impact Assessment* estimates that there will be administrative savings of at least £5 million a year when EMAs become fully operational in 2006. Applicants should find the process easier and there will be increased safeguards against fraud and loss of public monies.

## Section 109: unauthorised disclosure of information received under section 108

An offence is created for the unlawful disclosure of information received under s. 108 which, on conviction, can result in up to two years in prison or a fine or both. A defence can be that the person believed that the disclosure was lawful. Schools and colleges have an important role in deciding whether entitled students receive weekly EMA attendance payments and bonus payments through monitoring attendance. The new legislation does not affect this role, but schools and colleges have no role in determining eligibility. Therefore, school and college staff should not be in receipt of information provided by the Inland Revenue and DWP under s. 108 and should not be at risk of making an unauthorised disclosure. There is no role for LEAs in this process, except over attendance checking in school sixth forms. Local authorities will need to make applications on behalf of children in care although, again, this should not involve receipt of Inland Revenue or DWP information.

## Section 110: supply of information: free school lunches, etc.

Under ss. 512 to 512A of the Education Act 1996, FSM and, where provided, free milk are available to the children of families where a parent is in receipt of (i) income support, (ii) income-based jobseekers allowance, (iii) support provided under part 6 of the Immigration and Asylum Act 1999 or (iv) Child Tax Credit, provided that they do not also receive Working Tax Credit and that their annual income (as assessed by the Inland Revenue) does not exceed a figure determined annually.

In order to receive FSM and milk, a parent must apply to their LEA, either directly or, where delegated, to their child's school. Determining eligibility involves a local check on information originating from the Inland Revenue (Tax Credit Award Notice), DWP benefit records or immigration status. (There are no legislative barriers on the supply of Home Office information on immigration status for determining FSM eligibility under part 6 of the Immigration and Asylum Act 1999 to the DfES or local government.)

The *Regulatory Impact Assessment* estimates that schools will save £4.2 million and LEAs £2.1 million annually through small administration costs. Schools would no longer have to carry out eligibility checks. Instead, a simple form would be completed by the claimant and LEAs would submit the information to the DfES electronically. There would be no need to check complicated documents. The LEA would receive information about a family's eligibility but would not have access to Inland Revenue or DWP information. Human error would be reduced and fraud, through presenting forged documents, should be eliminated. The DfES hopes that electronic checking will encourage greater take-up of entitlement by reducing the possible stigma on claimants in having to take documents into schools and LEAs for checking.

Section 110 (1) to (3) allows for the electronic capture of data held by the Inland Revenue and DWP and for its transmission to the DfES for the purpose of determining eligibility for FSM and milk. The implicit assumption is that the DfES can ask only for information on specifically named individuals when requested by the LEA. Section 110(4) allows DWP information to be supplied directly to an LEA and s. 110(5) allows information held by the DfES to be shared with LEAs. Section 110(6) allows information to be passed to a contractor carrying out the eligibility checking function on behalf of an

LEA. Section 110(7) enables eligibility to be determined for pupils attending non-maintained special schools and academies.

## Section 111: unauthorised disclosure of information received under section 110

An offence is created for the unlawful disclosure of information received under s. 110 which, on conviction, can result in up to two years in prison or a fine or both. Section 111(1) gives the circumstances in which information may be lawfully disclosed, which includes functions relating to eligibility for FSM and milk. LEAs and schools will not be given detailed information about a person's tax or benefit status; only eligibility for free school meals will be disclosed. Care will need to be taken on how schools and LEAs use this information for statistical purposes and for collating the Schools Census return.

## Section 112: power to provide that function of determining eligibility remains with the LEA

Legislation under the SSFA 1998 allows LEA school lunch functions to be delegated to schools as determined by an order of the Secretary of State. Section 112 amends the order-making power in s. 512A of the 1996 Act (as substituted by the 1998 Act) to enable eligibility checks for free lunches, etc. to be returned to the LEA for schools that have had delegated responsibility. In other words, this section provides that, whilst LEAs can be required to delegate responsibility for school lunch provision, they cannot be required to delegate the responsibility for FSM eligibility checks. Where FSM checks have been delegated, the Secretary of State can order that the delegation be withdrawn.

## Section 113: information about the school workforce: introductory

Section 113 paves the way for the data collection provisions in s. 114. A 'qualifying worker' is someone who is an employee, or otherwise engaged to work at, a school, or provides education at a further education institution. This definition will cover schools and colleges in the independent sector. A 'qualifying worker' will also include individuals under contract of employment with, or otherwise contracted to, a children's services authority (CSA) to supply education or services. Sections 113 and 114 are the only mention of CSAs in the Act; this will enable data capture about staff that are employed under a local authority's children's social services functions or otherwise as well as those employed under LEA functions. Trainees may be included, although in practice this will not, for example, include students on full-time higher-education courses of ITT doing teaching practice.

In keeping with the title of the section, however, the Government's data collection strategy appears to be limited to collecting data on adults working in schools, performing teaching duties out of school, or performing direct support roles, rather than the whole children's workforce. The new data collection exercise will replace:

- the current Form 618g, the workforce section of Annual Schools Census
- the Secondary School Curriculum and Staffing Survey
- the Employers' Organisation Survey on Teacher Resignations and Recruitment
- the Office of Manpower Economics, Pay Survey.

Further information on which staff will be subject to information gathering can be found from the draft code-sets for the 'Contract Service Agreement module' of the School Workforce Level School Census published on the www.teachernet.gov.uk website.

## Section 114: supply of information about the school workforce

The first attempts to collect statistical information from schools electronically began about 20 years ago. Comprehensive information on pupils was achieved in 2002. The DfES believes this has led to a significant decrease in administrative burdens on schools and LEAs. The creation of the National Pupil Database with matched National Curriculum assessment information has supported national planning and research, as has the publication of the Assessment and Attainment tables. Information about pupils has supported a wide range of school improvement and administrative functions, such as performance benchmarking and allowing records to follow pupils when they transfer between schools. The Government is planning to roll out the first England-wide adult-level data collection in 2007 with a pilot in 2006.

Section 114(1) to (3) gives the Secretary of State wide regulation-making powers over who must supply information and the bodies that may receive information. School proprietors and Children's Services Authorities can be required to supply information. The school proprietor for a maintained school is the governing body. It is understood that the Government does not intend to extend adult-level school workforce data collection to the independent sector except for academies, CTCs and non-maintained special schools. Section 114(1)(c) enables the Secretary of State to prescribe other persons who can be required to supply information, but section 114(4)(a) limits the persons to those 'carrying out functions of a public nature', for example, a voluntary sector project educating children out of school. Section 114(2)(c) and 114(4)(a) enables the Secretary of State to prescribe other persons who can receive information provided that that person is exercising functions of a public nature. This will include other local government functions. The Secretary of State will be able to supply information to researchers where the research relates to education or training and where research may be expected to be of public benefit. Section 114 (5) lists the purposes for which information can be shared: evaluation, planning, research or statistical purposes. Additional purposes may also be prescribed in regulations. The *Explanatory Notes* give further information as follows.

*'Evaluation purposes' is intended to cover those situations where data are used internally by the organisation holding the data in order to formulate policy. For example, in relation to a policy to promote teacher retention in London schools by increasing pay, the database would be used to monitor whether this had been effective.*

*'Planning purposes' could cover the use of data to inform a teacher supply model, with the aim of ensuring that there are sufficient places available on relevant courses so that there are enough teachers with the right skills in schools.*

*'Research purposes' could cover a situation where researchers are studying the deployment of maths and science teachers in schools. At present researchers have to approach schools directly to find out who is teaching these subjects and what sort of qualifications they hold. The database would provide researchers with this information in advance to inform their research.*

*'Statistical purposes' covers situations where data are analysed and then statistics are produced and published in aggregate form.*

Section 114(6) allows the Secretary of State to make regulations to enable data sharing between organisations, such as CSAs, that are already lawfully allowed to hold, or be supplied with, that data. The *Explanatory Notes* give the following examples:

i)    *where a teacher moves to a new school and the school which the teacher has left should have passed information about that teacher to the new school but does not: the Department will to be able to supply that data to the new school*

ii)   *where a teacher moves to teach in a different local education authority, and the new local education authority are missing some data items on that teacher, such as his date of birth: the Department will be able to send the data to the local education authority directly rather than the new authority having to ask the teacher to fill in the missing information*

iii)  *where partner organisations such as the General Teaching Council for England*

---

*or Wales and Ofsted have existing powers to hold or be supplied with specified information on the school workforce, the Department will be able to supply that information directly to them.*

The Secretary of State can make regulations under s. 114(8) that will prevent persons from disclosing supplied information unless authorised to do so. It will also enable bodies to be compelled to give information through a court order that are in default of their obligation to supply information under s. 114.

# Attendance at alternative education provision

Sections 115 and 116 fill a gap in previous legislation. It will now be possible to compel the attendance of children at 'alternative provision', that is educational provision made by a governing body or LEA but not in a school, including provision in a Pupil Referral Unit (PRU). Often, such provision is in the voluntary and charitable sector.

## Section 115: power of the governing body to make alternative provision for excluded pupils

A seemingly minor change is made to section 29(3) of the Education Act 2002 (governing body power to require pupil attendance outside the school premises). This is an historic power that enables schools to require pupils, for example, to attend a sports field for physical education. Section 115 substitutes 'registered pupils' for 'pupils in attendance at the school' and enables a governing body to require a pupil who has been excluded for a fixed period, or has been permanently excluded and is awaiting an independent appeal, to attend alternative educational provision.

## Section 116: failure of a parent to secure regular school attendance of a child at alternative provision

A new s. 444ZA (application of section 444 to alternative educational provision) is inserted into the Education Act 1996. The new s. 444ZA extends the circumstances in which a parent or a carer can be prosecuted for failing to ensure that a child for whom he/she is responsible attends the alternative provision that has been made for the child. Non-attendance at a PRU is already covered by existing legislation. A penalty notice, as inserted into the 1996 Act by the Anti-social Behaviour Act 2003, can be issued as an alternative to prosecution. This is achieved in these circumstances by applying for a prosecution under s. 444 of the 1996 Act (offence: failure to secure regular attendance at school of registered pupil), which in turn enables the use of s. 444A (penalty notice in respect of failure to secure regular attendance at school of registered pupil) for a penalty notice.

The RIA argues that the extension of the ability to apply sanctions 'will act as an incentive for some children and their families to co-operate with efforts to provide an education', but that the powers should be exercised only 'when it appears appropriate to do so'. Of the 67,000 children in alternative provision, the RIA estimates that 737 will receive penalty notices or be prosecuted each year.

The following refers to the new section 444ZA inserted into the Education Act 1996. Subsection (1) applies to a child who is not registered at a school (which will include a PRU) but has had educational provision organised for him/her by the LEA otherwise than at a school. The LEA will be able to prosecute the parents or issue a penalty notice should these children not attend alternative provision made for them.

Subsections (2) and (3) apply to the case where a pupil who is excluded for a fixed period from a maintained school, or is still on the register awaiting an appeal following a permanent exclusion, is required by the governing body to attend alternative educational provision. If the pupil does not attend, the LEA can prosecute the parent or issue a penalty notice. The headteacher of the school from which the pupil has been excluded can also issue a penalty notice. See ss. (8) for the use of these powers by academies and CTCs.

Parents must be told in writing that the pupil must attend alternative provision. The notice can also be given by any other effective method (ss. 116(5)). Before any proceedings or notices are issued, the pupil must have failed to attend regularly (ss. (4)) after the parents were informed of the need to attend the alternative provision. Under ss. (6) a parent can claim that suitable education is being provided otherwise for the child as a defence against prosecution. Subsection (7) defines who may grant a pupil leave from alternative provision. These are persons 'authorised by the LEA' for arrangements made by the LEA, and the governing body for a maintained school. Subsection (8) defines 'relevant school' and includes academies and CTCs as well as schools maintained by LEAs (including PRUs) as schools that can require their pupils to attend alternative education provision.

Supplementary amendments are made in schedule 18 as follows:

- para. 1 amends s. 36 of the Children Act 1989 to include alternative provision in the scope of Education Supervision Orders

- para. 3 amends s. 444A of the Education Act 1996 to include alternative provision in the scope of penalty notices

- para. 6 amends s. 566 of the Education Act 1996 to enable the person in charge of the alternative provision to sign certificates of attendance required in any legal proceedings

- para. 15 amends s. 19 of the Anti-social Behaviour Act 2003 to include alternative provision in the scope of parenting contracts.

# Supplementary

## Section 117 and schedule 18: further amendments related to part 4

These contain supplementary and consequential provisions arising from the new provisions in part 4. See comment on sections 101, 103 and 116 (earlier) for further information.

## Section 118: meaning of 'the 2002 Act' in part 4

The term 'the 2002 Act' is a reference to the Education Act 2002, which is frequently amended in this part of the Education Act 2005.

# Part 5  General

Part 5 contains general provisions about the use of the Secretary of State's powers to make subordinate legislation (that is regulations and orders), general interpretation, repeals, commencement and extent.

## Section 119: functions to be exercisable by the National Assembly for Wales

This section applies to Wales only.

## Section 120: subordinate legislation: general provisions

This section requires orders or regulations to be made by a statutory instrument that in England will require the instrument to be 'laid' before Parliament. Regulations about school inspection can name particular schools or categories of schools.

## Section 121: parliamentary control of subordinate legislation

This section enables any statutory instrument laid by the Secretary of State under this Act to be annulled by a resolution of one or other of the Houses of Parliament. The exceptions are commencement orders under s. 125 where orders cannot be annulled, and regulations under s. 124 where an affirmative resolution of both Houses is required. See also the notes on s. 101 in part 4 for an amendment to the order-making powers in the SSFA 1998 on school funding (page 54).

## Section 122: general interpretation

This section contains the rules for interpreting amendments by the 2005 Act to earlier education legislation. Where relevant, these changes have been explained at the relevant point in this Digest.

## Section 123 and schedule 19: repeals

This section lists the repeals of other legislation contained in the 2005 Act. Major repeals are listed at the relevant point in this Digest.

## Section 124: power to make further supplementary and consequential provision, etc.

This section enables the Secretary of State to make regulations 'to make such supplementary, incidental, consequential, transitional, transitory or saving provision' to any provision in the Act other than the technical provisions in part 5. In order to change an Act of Parliament, the proposal must be approved by resolution of each House of Parliament. The *Explanatory Notes* justify this power – known as a Henry VII power – because the changes made to the law on school funding and school organisation in particular 'affect complex areas of education legislation', and it is likely that consequential amendments may be required 'that cannot reasonably be anticipated'.

## Section 125: commencement

This section brought a few provisions into force on Royal Assent (7 April 2005). These include:

- the interpretation of certain terms
- definitions in ss. 75 and 78 relating to the training of the school workforce
- ss. 96, 97 and 100 concerning training, institutions of a denominational character, and the interpretation of certain terms to do with training the school workforce.

The Act also brings into force two months after Royal Assent (7 Jun 2005):

- s. 102 on the requirement for LEAs in England to set annual targets
- s. 107 and schedule 17 on restrictions on disposal of land
- ss. 108 to 112 on sharing of information for the administration of Education Maintenance Allowances and FSM
- ss. 113 and 114 on the supply of information about the school workforce.

Regulations are required before ss. 102 and 114 become operative. At the time of writing (June 2005), the Government had not published a general commencement order. See the section on 'Implementing the Act' in the Introduction to this Digest for further information (page xvii).

## Section 126: the appropriate authority by whom the commencement order is made

This section states whether the Secretary of State or the Welsh Assembly is responsible for commencing which section of the Act.

## Section 127: extent

This section explains that the Act applies to England and Wales except that the provision on education maintenance the allowances (ss. 108 and 109) applies to Scotland and Northern Ireland as well as England and Wales.

## Section 128: short title, etc.

This section enables the Education Act 2005 to be treated as an 'Education Act' for the convenience of common definitions.

# References

CLARKE, C. (2004). *Clarke Congratulates Teacher Training Agency and Announces Enhanced Role* (DfES News 29 March 2004) [online]. Available: http://www.dfes.gov.uk/pns/DisplayPN.cgi?pn_id=2004_0046 [21 June, 2005].

DEPARTMENT FOR EDUCATION AND EMPLOYMENT (2001). *Code of Practice on Local Education Authority – School Relations* (DfEE 0027/2001). London: DfEE.

DEPARTMENT FOR EDUCATION AND SKILLS (2002). *Schools Causing Concern: Overview*. London: DfES.

DEPARTMENT FOR EDUCATION AND SKILLS (2003). *School Admissions Code of Practice*. London: DfES.

DEPARTMENT FOR EDUCATION AND SKILLS (2004a). *Department for Education and Skills: Five Year Strategy for Children and Learners* (Cm. 6272). London: The Stationery Office.

DEPARTMENT FOR EDUCATION AND SKILLS (2004b). *School Profile Consultation: Consultation Document*. London: DfES.

DEPARTMENT FOR EDUCATION AND SKILLS (2005a). *Children and Young People's Plan: Guidance on the Children and Young People's Plan* [online]. Available: http://www.dfes.gov.uk/consultations/downloadableDocs/Online%20Consultation%20Document.doc [1 July, 2005].

DEPARTMENT FOR EDUCATION AND SKILLS (2005b). *Explanatory Notes: Education Act 2005. Chapter 18*. London: The Stationery Office.

DEPARTMENT FOR EDUCATION AND SKILLS and OFFICE FOR STANDARDS IN EDUCATION (2004a). *A New Relationship with Schools*. London: DfES.

DEPARTMENT FOR EDUCATION AND SKILLS and OFFICE FOR STANDARDS IN EDUCATION (2004b). *A New Relationship with Schools: Improving Performance through School Self-Evaluation*. London: DfES.

DEPARTMENT FOR EDUCATION AND SKILLS and OFFICE FOR STANDARDS IN EDUCATION (2005). *A New Relationship with Schools: Next Steps*. London: DfES.

FOWLER, J. with EVANS, E. (2002). *A Guide to the Education Act 2002*. London: Advisory Centre for Education and The Education Network.

GREAT BRITAIN. PARLIAMENT. HOUSE OF COMMONS. EDUCATION AND SKILLS COMMITTEE (2004). *Secondary Education: School Admissions* (HC 58-1). London: The Stationery Office.

GREAT BRITAIN. PARLIAMENT. HOUSE OF COMMONS LIBRARY (2005). *The Education Bill (HL): Bill 77 of 2004–05* (Research Paper 05/20) [online]. Available: http://www.parliament.uk/commons/lib/research/rp2005/rp05-020.pdf [1 July, 2005].

OFFICE FOR STANDARDS IN EDUCATION (2004). *The Future of Inspection: a Consultation Paper* (HMI 2057). London: OFSTED.

OFFICE FOR STANDARDS IN EDUCATION (2005a). *Inspecting Schools: the Framework for Inspecting Schools in England from September 2005* (HMI 2435) [online]. Available: http://www.ofsted.gov.uk/publications/index.cfm?fuseaction=pubs.displayfile&id=3861&type=pdf [20 June, 2005].

OFFICE FOR STANDARDS IN EDUCATION (2005b). *Ofsted's New Inspection Arrangements* (Ofsted News 8 April) [online]. Available: http://www.ofsted.gov.uk/news/index.cfm?fuseaction=news.details&id=1685 [20 June, 2005].

WATERMAN, C. and FOWLER, J. (2004). *Plain Guide to the Children Act 2004*. Slough: NFER.

WHITBOURN, S. with MORRIS, R., PARKER, A., McDONOGH, K., FOWLER, J., MITCHELL, K. and POOLE, K. (2004). *What is the LEA for? An Analysis of the Functions and Roles of the Local Education Authority*. Second edn. Slough: EMIE at NFER.

# Glossary

| | |
|---|---|
| AI | additional inspectors |
| BSF | Building Schools for the Future |
| CPD | Continuing Professional Development |
| CSA | Children's Services Authority |
| CSCI | Commission for Social Care Inspection |
| CTC | City Technology College |
| DfES | Department for Education and Skills |
| DSG | Dedicated Schools Grant |
| DWP | Department for Work and Pensions |
| EMA | Education Maintenance Allowance |
| HEFCE | Higher Education Funding Council for England |
| HEFCW | Higher Education Funding Council for Wales |
| HMCI | Her Majesty's Chief Inspector of Schools |
| HMI | Her Majesty's Inspector of Schools |
| HLTA | Higher Level Teaching Assistant |
| ITT | Initial Teacher Training |
| LEA | Local education authority |
| LSC | Learning and Skills Council (p.29) |
| PRU | Pupil Referral Unit |
| RIA | Regulatory Impact Assessment |
| RISP | Regional Inspection Service Providers |
| SEF | self evaluation form |
| SFSS | Schools Formula Spending Share |
| SIA 1996 | School Inspections Act 1996 |
| SIP | School Improvement Partner |
| SOC | School Organisation Committee |

| SSFA 1998 | School Standards and Framework Act 1998 |
| TDA | Training and Development Agency for Schools |
| TTA | Teacher Training Agency |